COGNITIVE

BEHAVIORAL

THERAPY

11 Simple CBT Techniques to Strengthen Self-Awareness and Combat Negativity

Michael B. Stump

The Mentor Bucket

TABLE OF CONTENTS

Preface.. 1

Introduction 9

Chapter One: Mental-Health Issues and the Role of Cognitive Behavioral Therapy (CBT) 13

Chapter Two: Safety Plan 35

Chapter Three: Technique 1– Cognitive Restructuring 45

Chapter Four: Technique 2 – Bursting Mental Distortions.. 55

Chapter Five: Technique 3 – Write it Down.......... 75

Chapter Six: Technique 4 – Exposure and Response Prevention... 86

Chapter Seven: Technique 5 – Relax..................... 99

Chapter Eight: Technique 6 – Have Fun 116

Chapter Nine: Technique 7 – Testing the Beliefs 124

Chapter Ten: Technique 8 – Role-Playing 132

Chapter Eleven: Technique 9 – Simply Break It Down.. 142

Chapter Twelve: Technique 10 – Mindfulness..... 150

Chapter Thirteen: Technique 11 – Play the Entire Script.. 161

Final Words... 167

Preface

As usual, I was awake at the crack of dawn. If my mind had been clear, I would have appreciated the quietness of the morning, the fresh air and the beauty that comes with the first light of the day. However, I did not want to get out of bed. No, I wasn't sleepy. I could not even remember the last night I had had more than a few hours of sleep despite being in bed by 9:30 p.m. each night.

That Wednesday morning should have been an exciting day for me. I was finally receiving the award for being the top CEO in the pharmaceutical industry. I should have been excited and proud for accomplishing such a feat at only 38 years old. I was at the top of the world, leading the most promising and innovative company in the country, yet there I was, sad and crushed.

I glanced at my wife who was doing her yoga on a mat on the balcony. I couldn't help but appreciate her beauty yet notice that the joy and light in her were fading. She was a bubbly girl, confident and ambitious with sparkling eyes. What remained now was a shell of the woman I met and married. She looked in my direction and upon seeing me, looked away. The few seconds that our eyes met, I saw the heartbreak, the suppressed anger and hatred.

I knew that look; I had lived through that look. It was the same look my mother had when she looked at my father. For a moment, the world stood still, my eyes opened, and my mind was clear. I walked to the mirror and looked at myself. What had I become? My wife hated me, my children feared me, yet, on the outside, I was the most celebrated man. As I looked keenly at my face, I noticed my hollow eyes devoid of any emotion, I hated myself.

On the day I was to receive a prestigious award, the day I had the stamp of success, and the day I had a dinner invitation from the president, I felt worthless. I felt empty and broken inside. Most times, when I felt weak, I would focus my energy on my work or anger. Anger gave me the strength I needed. For once in my life, I did not yield to anger; there wasn't enough left within me.

As I sat on the edge of the bed, tears began rolling down my cheeks. My heart broke, my life seemed empty as a lie. Only one question was on my mind: "How did I get here?"

My mind went to that young energetic boy running in the fields, feeling free. He could hear his mother calling for him to go home have a meal. She did not have to call twice. Her food had a reputation in the village of being the best. As he approached the house, he could see his sisters helping to set the table while his younger brother played on the mat. Just as the last fork found its place on the dinner table, he heard his father pull up the drive. The entire household seemed to run outside to welcome the man of the house. They all looked forward to their father's arrival. Not only were there gifts but also stories and an evening filled with laughter and counsel.

Everything changed one evening. Father came home, but there were no stories or gifts, everything was solemn, and the young boy knew that something had changed. He, however, could not expect the magnitude of the change.

I quickly collected my thoughts, wiped away my tears and went into the bathroom to get ready for the day. Standing in the shower, I let the water flow and wash my feelings off, cleanse me of the burden I carried and make me free. Almost half an hour later I heard a soft knock on the door, I knew that my wife was wondering why I was taking so long. I was known as a stickler for time, and everything had to happen at a particular time, otherwise, there would be hell to pay if my tea was not at the right temperature.

At the office, everyone was excited about the award. Despite the excitement, there was something in the air, the same thing I felt at home: fear and tension. The staff came forward to offer congratulatory messages, but I kicked everyone out. I could not take it anymore. On my magnificent table, I broke down for the first time in years. I bared my soul, I felt so little, defeated, heavy, lost and alone...alone among hundreds of people. I sent a text to my wife asking her to come. She did not respond, and I knew I had pushed her away too.

In the bottom cabinet, there were some pills, the ones Dr. Elena gave me to help me calm down and, after the first two, I decided I needed more calm today than any other day. Filling my hand with the white pills, I drowned them with the waiting cup of tea and relaxed waiting for the calmness to set in. After all, it was better to end it all and have a peaceful life.

When I came to, I saw my wife seated beside me crying. She still looked beautiful, and I couldn't help but tell her. Relief filled her face as she called for the doctor. She held my hand throughout the examination and repeatedly whispered that everything could be OK. The doctor recommended that I go for therapy, which I adamantly refused. Therapy was for the weak.

Upon discharge, my wife took me home. That evening, she served the tea outside in the garden. It was a beautiful day. She looked into my eyes with concern and said she was listening. The girl can be stubborn when not scared. She urged me to talk to her and let out the devils within. The brokenness within me rose again.

With tears streaming from my eyes, I told her of my dad losing his job and slowly sinking into fits of anger. He felt incapable of taking care of us and instead of looking for something to do, another job, he accumulated anger at the world. He became a closet drunkard but maintained a face outside. My mother's family stepped in and set up a sweets shop for her, which my father claimed ownership, but hardly ever helped. With my mother taking care of the bills, my father got even angrier. He may have felt inadequate. That is when the abuse began. He would hit my mother so hard we were forced to go help her, lest he killed her. We were not spared of the beatings, either. He kept warning us to stay away from his fights with my mother.

The more I grew, the more I could not watch my mother get battered and my father praised for being an influential person in the community. I vowed to work hard and have so much money that I would never be like him. I focused my energy on school, made good grades and landed a scholarship. My mother and I were grateful, and she knew there was hope for the family.

One day I came home from the university and, as usual, my father, in his angry drunken state, descended on my mother with kicks and blows for serving him a cold dinner. I got in between them and, in the process, pushed him. He fell to the ground and hurt his head. He said that he would get his revenge. In the morning, mother did not wake up...it was all my fault.

We sat there, in the garden seat, sobbing. My wife hugged me and asked me why I carried that around for all those years. I told her I felt guilty for the death of my mother and, as a man, society did not allow me to show emotion or even talk about such things. Talking about pain and crying were for the weak. Men did not do so. She urged me to go for therapy and would walk through the journey with me. Although doubtful, I agreed. I was tired of being sick, tired, guilty and angry.

Initially, I thought therapy to be a waste of time. However, over time I have found myself. Having to look deep inside you will open your eyes to life as is. I have gotten an opportunity to face the pain inside me and chart the path for my life from a place of peace. I no longer need sleeping pills as the nightmares are gone. I have become a present father and a loving husband. I am still successful, and my business is growing each day thanks to me being more accommodating. I now receive innovative ideas from my staff without them worrying about being shouted at. I have gotten time to properly mourn for my mother and forgive my father. I chose not to give my father the space to turn me into him. I have control of my emotions and am no longer depressed. I am reborn.

Throughout my therapy, I realized that anyone can battle any form of mental illness. There is no particular way that people with depression or anxiety look. I was the successful, depressed CEO who never showed any signs of weakness, yet I was sick. I have met happy people who cry themselves to sleep. Most importantly, I have practically learned about different ways that you can apply to defeat mental issues, like depression and anxiety. I did it, and you can do it, too!

Having been there and successfully gone through therapy despite having been in denial and feeling lost and hopeless, I am willing to share with you what worked for me. I must confess that prior to Cognitive Behavioral Therapy (CBT), I went through other forms of treatment, including medication, but that did not help. I felt worse once the effect of the pills wore off, and it was through that medication that I saw a way to end my life. My journey through CBT was not easy in the beginning. Having to look inside was especially difficult, but I learned, walked the path and healed. I can help you get the peace and healing you crave. Together, we can walk from the depths of hopelessness and darkness and into the light and hope. I will offer simple and practical techniques that you can apply as part of your daily activities to ensure that you get better, find your peace and cement your place in the society. I am looking forward to the emergence of a strong, confident and positive person who spreads joy and peace to those around him—that is you.

Introduction

We all have some dark days when we lack energy and feel down. You must have experienced that, especially, in these challenging times and the economy slumping. Those days are the worst; even interacting with other people is tiresome. Now, consider feeling like this every other day and having to carry on with life? Sad as it is, it is what is happening to millions of people all over the world. The World Health Organization in 2019 estimated that 264 million people globally were depressed. Please note this was before the pandemic and that is depression only. In total, about 790 million people in the world suffer from one form of mental disorder or another.

Yet, mental health is not considered as important as physical health. If you hurt your leg today, the entire family would drive you to the emergency room. On the other hand, if they saw you slowly slipping away, moody and losing interest in life, they would assume that you would simply snap back. The only time most people will take action is when physical evidence appears, such as wounds from self-hurt or hurting others. As a society, we want to see evidence that the other person is sick, something like fever or convulsion. We are convinced that the smiling girl cannot be sick or the high-flying athlete cannot be depressed. How can they be sick when they are so beautiful, energetic and successful? Despite signs, like unexplainable mood swings, panic attacks and visible anxiety, mental illness is not accorded the necessary weight.

Have you been battling any form of mental illness? Do you have someone close to you going through depression or anxiety? Well, no matter how misunderstood you feel, you can have some peace in the knowledge that you are not alone. I have been there, and although my situation may be different from yours, I pulled through, and so can you.

In this book, we look at the overview of mental health and some of the mental illnesses that are increasing each day. The focus, however, will be on the techniques that you can apply to deal with mental issues. In particular, we will look at simple techniques, such as journaling and testing your beliefs. The aim of this book is to help you go through the process, even at home. I will offer practical advice, in a simple manner, on some of the methods that I used in my journey that proved to be effective.

If you or someone you know needs to face the muddy grounds within them, to address those underlying issues, swim through the murky waters to the clean water, then this is the book. There is no need to wallow in pain anymore. You do not have to keep being weighed down by what you carry; you can offload and have some rest. Don't bother picking up that baggage again; you can throw it away and enjoy the life that you are blessed to have. Joy and peace are for everyone, not a chosen few. Not only can you have life, but life in abundance.

You are not alone. This book is for you who feels like you are carrying the weight of the world on your shoulders. It is particularly tailored for you who feel those suicidal thoughts creeping in and feel so overwhelmed and powerless. Yet, this book is also for that person that feels down and has yet to pin it down to a reason. Whatever mental issue you are facing, this book is a resource to take you step by step through the healing and self-discovery process using simple cognitive behavioral therapy techniques. In addition to these, the book also targets caregivers to help them give care and hope to the mentally ill. They say information is power.

Being equipped with the information in this book not only contributes to their improved knowledge but places them in a better position to deal with their patients.

The time to cry yourself to sleep is over. Now is not the time to entertain those harmful thoughts. You can get out of this. You can breathe again and enjoy life. Yes, you can be in control of your mind and actions.

"The happiness of your life depends on the quality of your thoughts."
— Marcus Aurelius

Chapter One

Mental-Health Issues and the Role of Cognitive Behavioral Therapy (CBT)

For a long time, therapy was a reserve of a few people who were mainly considered to be 'mad'. Having to see a therapist meant that you were losing your mind, or you were a weakling. Normal people faced and dealt with issues. They went through hiding any mental issues because society was not prepared to handle them. However, over the years, mental-health issues have begun to gain recognition and be treated as illnesses rather than a weakness.

The challenge with mental illnesses is that they are not easy to detect. I am certain that everyone at one point or another has experienced anxiety. Times like right before an interview, while waiting for results, on a first date, or when experiencing other illnesses. Most of us get panic attacks once in a while, and those blue days do come. Sometimes it's a whole week that is blue or even several weeks. At what point is it just a bad day, and when does it graduate to a health concern? Let us see what is normal, then we can tell what is abnormal.

Mental Health

Each day you wake up, you can expect to feel, think and act. How you do so is determined by the state of your mental health. If two people are hurt by someone, one may complain and walk away while another may draw a gun and shoot. How healthy your mental health is determines how well you can make choices, handle stress and relate to other people. Therefore, mental health is your psychological, social and emotional well-being.

Taking care of your mental health is important at each stage of life, be it childhood, adolescence or adulthood. If anything happens at any point in life that destabilizes the wellness of the mind, you could start experiencing mental-health problems. You cannot outgrow mental-health issues. As you live and feel pity or judge others who have such issues, remember that you are not past them. Each day presents the potential for joining millions of people suffering from mental-health disorders. Do not worry though; it is now easier to detect mental disorders and even to treat them. Besides, you can put in measures to prevent mental-health issues.

If you have the bubbly and outgoing neighbour who now hardly goes out or even bothers to shower, you must wonder how she got there. Well, there are many factors that contribute to mental-health problems. Some of these include:

- Life experiences like abuse, loss, or trauma
- Biological factors like brain chemistry or genes
- Family history: People who come from lineages of people with mental-health problems are inclined to develop similar problems.

What are mental-health disorders?

They are also referred to as mental-health illnesses, and they include a wide range of conditions that affect your behavior, mood or thinking. Some of the most common ones include anxiety disorders, depression, addictive behaviors, eating disorders and schizophrenia.

While it is normal to experience mental-health concerns from time to time, it becomes an illness when the signs and symptoms result in frequent stress and hinder your ability to function. Experiencing anxiety because of a test or a problem does not translate to a mental disorder. However, when the anxiety becomes so frequent that you can no longer undertake your daily activities with ease, then there is a problem.

Mental-health disorders have the ability to make your life a living hell. They can make you unproductive, dirty and unable to form and sustain relationships with others. They can ruin your family and career. Signs and symptoms of different disorders vary from one person to another and come in varying intensities.

Who is suffering?

If you are suffering from one or more mental-health disorders, you may be a difficult person to please, but at least have some peace in the knowledge that you are not alone. The World Bank estimates that at least 10% of the people in the world are affected. Furthermore, about 20% of children and adolescents have to deal with some type of mental illness. Countries that have violence and conflict have an estimated 22% of their population suffering from mental disorders.

Depression is the major mental-health disorder and affects about 264 million people, with a majority of them being women, as per a WHO report in 2019. About 54 million people suffer from bipolar disorder, 20 million are affected by schizophrenia and a further 50 million people have dementia. You can tell from the data that mental disorders are not a preserve of a few. Sadly, the population of people suffering from these illnesses is increasing due to economic factors and the changing times.

Are you affected?

Many people suffer for a long time from mental disorders before they are diagnosed and put on treatment. In my case, I had to reach a breaking point to take action. The challenge is that the symptoms are attributable to life's pressures and normal feelings and that makes it difficult to point them out. If you are unsure, here are some of the common symptoms of mental illnesses. Please note that these can vary from person to person as per the circumstances and disorder.

Many people with mental-health problems experience sadness or feeling down, reduced ability to concentrate, confused thinking and extreme mood swings. They can be over the moon one moment and completely broken the next. Excessive worries and fears are common, as well as withdrawal from activities and friends. If you have that one friend who is suddenly very busy even for coffee, you may want to check up on him.

Other symptoms include low energy, tiredness and sleep problems, as well as an inability to deal with stress and daily problems, which can lead to hallucinations, paranoia and detachment from reality. The person may also experience trouble relating to people and situations or become hostile, angry and violent. You may also notice changes in eating habits and sex drives, as well as destructive thoughts. Mental disorders may be accompanied by alcohol and drug use. There is more. Occasionally, the person may experience physical problems, like back pain, stomach pains and headaches.

Looking at all these symptoms that zap the life out of a person, it is evident that mental illnesses deserve to be taken seriously. If you or a person close to you are exhibiting one of these symptoms, it is best to see your physician or a mental-health professional. Most mental illnesses get worse if left untreated, and it is best to get an early diagnosis. If things seem thick, and you feel like you're on the verge of harming yourself or others, don't be like me. Call 911 or any emergency number. Remember that no matter how bad you are feeling, your life matters.

Diagnosis of Mental illness

Often the people affected by mental illness do not realize that they have a problem because most of the symptoms are feelings we all experience, like anger, sadness and anxiety. Therefore, when a person begins to note increased frequency and intensity of these symptoms, it is best to go for diagnosis.

The diagnosis process may involve a physical exam to ensure that the symptoms are not caused by a physical problem. Laboratory tests are also done to ensure the proper functioning of the body system. Lab tests may include screening for drugs or thyroid function, among others. Finally, a psychological evaluation is done. The health practitioner talks to the patient about thoughts, feelings, symptoms and behavior patterns.

Most mental illnesses display a similar array of symptoms, and it may be an uphill task to get the right diagnosis. There is a need to take time and effort in digging deeper into the symptoms, thoughts and behavior patterns to get the right diagnosis.

Treatment Methods

If diagnosis shows that there is a mental disorder, the preferred method of treatment will depend on the mental illness in question, how severe it is and what works best for you. I know some people who can barely swallow a pill, yet others even go a step ahead to self-medicate and abuse pills. There is also the question of how controllable the condition is, which will determine the treatment team to bring on board. For example, if you are suffering from something mild, you can undergo the treatment by yourself. However, if you have, for instance, been diagnosed with Type 1 Bipolar, then your treatment team may need to be larger than your primary care provider.

A holistic treatment team includes the primary care doctor, nurse, physician assistant, psychiatrist, pharmacist, psychotherapist, social worker and family members. You remain to be the most important member of this team.

Ideally, you should be presented with different options available for treatment and, together with the health care professional, choose one that suits you best. Whatever method you settle for, ensure that you fully understand all the benefits and risks that come with it. Some of the available methods include:

1. Medications

With mental illnesses, medications are hardly ever curative. Instead, they help to alleviate the severity of the symptoms. For example, if you are suffering from Post-Traumatic Stress Disorder and cannot sleep due to recurring nightmares, you can be given sleeping pills to help you sleep better. However, these pills do not address the trauma that is causing a lack of sleep.

Do not think that you will not need medications. They help to improve the effectiveness of other treatment methods, like psychotherapy. Some of the medications used are:

- Antidepressants, for anxiety, depression and related conditions.
- Mood-stabilizing medications that help with bipolar disorders.
- Anti-anxiety medications that treat panic attacks and anxiety disorders.
- Antipsychotic medications for conditions, like schizophrenia and also help with bipolar disorders and depression.

2. Residential/Hospital Treatment Programs

In some cases, the mental illness is so severe that you have to be put in a psychiatric hospital for care. If you are a danger to yourself and others, it becomes necessary to have you admitted for around-the-clock care.

3. Brain-stimulus treatment

Some mental illnesses can be stubborn or the person suffering from them is so stubborn that medications and even psychotherapy do not work. These conditions that are determined to make their home and protect it at all costs are dealt with using brain stimuli. The patient may undergo electroconvulsive therapy, deep brain stimulation, vagus nerve stimulation or repetitive transcranial magnetic stimulation.

4. Substance-abuse treatment

As mentioned earlier, some of the mental illnesses stem from the abuse of alcohol and drugs. In other cases, the mental disorder can push someone to start abusing drugs in a bid to deal with the symptoms. At times, you can find someone with a social disorder taking a shot or two of tequila to calm his nerves down. Over time, this becomes a norm and, since the anxiety is always there when has to go for social events, he quickly becomes addicted. Even for those on other treatment methods, the intake of alcohol and drugs interferes with their success. Specialized treatment for substance abuse is therefore offered to the patient.

5. Psychotherapy

In psychotherapy sessions, you talk to a mental-health professional about your condition and learn more about it. Some people call it **Talk Therapy** or collaborative treatment. With this understanding and the insights gained, it becomes easy to learn about coping strategies and skills to manage stress. Besides, since the sessions take a few months, it provides time to adjust. In some cases, there is a need for long-term treatment. The good thing with psychotherapy is that you can have sessions in groups to learn from others or even include your support people, like family.

There are different psychotherapy treatment plans that you can choose from that are Empirically Supported Treatments (ESTs) are:

- *Psychodynamic Psychotherapy* focuses on improving awareness of unconscious behaviors and thoughts, conflict resolution, and the development of new insights into various motivations.
- *Supportive Psychotherapy* emphasizes your coping abilities with stress and other difficult situations.

- ***Cognitive Behavioral Therapy (CBT)*** helps in the identification of unhealthy negative behaviors and beliefs and helps to replace these with positive and healthy ones.

<u>In this book, we will focus on Cognitive Behavioral Therapy, one of the most effective treatment plans for depression and anxiety, as well as intuitive thoughts. CBT boasts as the most effective psychological method of treating both moderate and severe depression.</u>

Having personally gone through CBT for intrusive thoughts and depression, I can confidently endorse this method as having great success. Besides, you have the option of having a support system to walk through the journey with you. CBT provides simple techniques that you can practice with ease to get good results.

What is Cognitive Behavioral Therapy?

CBT is one of the psychotherapeutic treatments that helps you identify disturbing, destructive and undesired thought patterns that negatively influence emotions and behavior. When you know what ails you, it is now possible to change these patterns and develop positive behavior and emotions.

Over the years, CBT has been extensively used in the treatment of most mental illnesses, including anxiety, depression, eating disorders, severe mental disorders, as well as problems associated with alcohol and drug use. Evidence from research studies show that CBT is more effective than psychiatric medications or other kinds of psychological therapy. CBT can even help in the management of marital problems. You don't have to trust me; just try it for yourself. Additionally, engaging in Cognitive Behavioral Therapy has a way of improving the functioning and quality of your life. You do not only get psychologically well but also live a great and fulfilling life, all thanks to CBT.

You can relax in the knowledge that the advances made in CBT over the years have been based on both clinical practice and research. There is no trial and error. In addition to having successfully gone through the process and seen positive results, there is much scientific evidence to show that this form of therapy produces positive change.

Core Principles of CBT

Some of the most important principles that form the basis for CBT include:

- Unhelpful or faulty ways of thinking form the foundation for psychological problems.

- Unhelpful behavior or learned patterns also form the basis of psychological problems.
- Those affected by psychological problems can learn better coping strategies that help to relieve their symptoms and help them to live more effective lives.

CBT employs different strategies in an effort to change thinking patterns, such as:

- Learning to identify the distortions in your thinking that are causing problems and then re-looking at them from a reality point of view.
- Developing a clearer understanding of the behavior, as well as the behavior of others.
- Learning to use problem-solving skills when faced with a difficult situation.
- Gaining greater self-confidence in your abilities.

When working on a change in behavioral patterns, some CBT strategies that are helpful include:

- Instead of avoiding or running away from your fears, you face them head on.
- Preparation is key. You can prepare for those difficult and problematic interactions with

others by role-playing so you can boost your confidence in handling similar situations.

- Learning to relax the body and calm the mind down so you do not overreact and behave in an inappropriate manner.

Unlike other modes of treatment, CBT allows you and the psychologist to work together collaboratively to clearly understand the problem and come up with a workable treatment strategy. In a way, you learn to be your own therapist through the exercises you engage in during sessions as well as the take-home work that you do. Unlike medication that is reliant on an external source of help, CBT helps you to look within you to find the answers that you need and draw the necessary strength to carry forward.

Ultimately, CBT is based on your current life. Some of the challenges you are facing may be drawn from your past, and it is important to acknowledge that part of your life. However, CBT does not give much emphasis on the past but rather the present. The target here is to ensure that you move forward in life by developing effective ways of coping.

Some of the common mental disorders

Anxiety Disorders

If you experience distressing and frequent apprehension and fear, you are likely to be suffering from an anxiety disorder. We all feel anxious from time to time especially in stressful situations. However, when you have an anxiety disorder, you tend to feel so even during non-stressful situations. The bouts may go for long periods of time, sometimes even half a year at a time.

The term 'anxiety disorders' refers to a number of conditions, including:

Obsessive Compulsive Disorder (OCD)

OCD is a mental condition that causes a person to have repeated unwanted sensations or thoughts (obsessions). The person may also have the urge to keep doing something over and over (compulsions). For example, a person can have an obsessive thought that some numbers are bad or have the compulsion to check the locks about three times each night or wash their hands five times after touching anything dirty. Although we all have certain habits that we keep repeating, having OCD means that these actions and thoughts are not enjoyable, take up more than an hour every day, are beyond one's control, and interfere with life, be it the work or social part of it. The four general categories of OCD include:

- *Contamination*: You fear possibly dirty things and have a compulsion to clean. You may also experience mental contamination where you feel like you are being treated like dirt.
- *Checking*: Repeated checking of locks, switches, systems or even medical conditions or pregnancy. Picture someone who conducts a pregnancy test every few days because they think they may be pregnant.
- *Intrusive thoughts and ruminations*: Here, you become obsessed with a particular line of thought, and some thoughts are disturbing or violent.
- *Symmetry and order*: You want all things lined up in a certain way. Some people go as far as arranging their cereals according to color.

Post-Traumatic Stress Disorder (PTSD)

When you have been through a terrifying event, like war or a fire, there is the possibility of developing a mental-health condition. The common symptoms include nightmares, flashbacks, uncontrollable thoughts about the traumatic event and severe anxiety.

Anyone who goes through a traumatic event will have difficulty coping and adjusting to life, but over time and with good care, it is possible to get better. In some cases, the trauma is so much that the symptoms keep getting worse and can last for months or years, making it difficult to live a full life. When the traumatic event hinders you from functioning normally, you may have Post-Traumatic Stress Disorder.

Panic Disorder

You may have panic disorder if you experience recurring but unanticipated panic attacks. Panic is the intense discomfort or fear that rises to a peak within minutes. The problem with panic disorder is that the people suffering from it tend to live in fear of having an attack, which makes them tense and consequently increases their chance of having one. Visualize a situation where you fear failure so much that you live in fear of failing only to end up failing. That sounds more complicated than it is.

Symptoms of panic disorder include sweating, breathing difficulties and a racing heart. In essence, you feel like the world is falling apart without any warning, suffocating or choking.

Social Anxiety Disorder

Have you ever had butterflies on a first date? Or felt them flapping their wings just before you start an important presentation? You have nothing to worry about; that is part of life, but not for everyone. Some people suffer from social phobia also called social anxiety disorder. For them, everyday interactions are a cause of significant anxiety, embarrassment, self-consciousness and fear. They are afraid of being judged or scrutinized by others and opt to avoid others as much as possible leading to a disruption in their daily activities.

People with social phobia worry about embarrassing themselves and that others will notice their anxiety. They will therefore avoid being the center of attention, avoid speaking for fear of embarrassment, and even get anxious at the thought of meeting others or being in a socially involved event. Physical symptoms include trembling, sweating, blushing, muscle tension, dizziness, nausea and trouble catching their breath. If you experience social phobia, you may find your mind going blank when someone asks you even a simple question.

Generalized Anxiety Disorder (GAD)

Having GAD means that you have an uncontrollable worry about common situations and occurrences. Some people refer to it as chronic anxiety neurosis. Often, we worry about one thing or another, particularly finances, but if you have GAD, you will worry several times daily for many months even when there is nothing to worry about. Sometimes you may not even know what you are worrying about except feeling that something bad may happen. At this point, the worry takes over your life, and it affects your daily activities and relationships with others.

Symptoms of GAD include sleep problems, poor concentration, irritability, shaking, rapid heartbeat, sweaty palms, muscle tension and even diarrhoea. All that worrying can be tiresome, resulting in fatigue and exhaustion.

You are likely to get GAD if you have family members with anxiety, faced abuse in childhood, take excessive caffeine or tobacco that escalates existing anxiety, and are exposed to stressful situations for a long time.

Mood Disorders

There is a saying that says, "Not every day is Sunday", meaning that days vary, and each day brings with it different tidings. We all experience mood swings. At least one in every 10 adults suffers from a type of mood disorder that disrupts their lives. If you are among them, you will have severe and persistent symptoms that make life difficult. The symptoms vary as per the specific disorder, but generally they include excessive guilt, feeling hopeless, low self-esteem and reduced energy.

Psychotic Disorders

People suffering from psychotic disorders lose their sense of reality such that they can't tell what is real and what is not. Some contributing factors to this disorder include certain viruses' trauma, extreme stress, drug abuse, and the working (or lack of working) of specific brain circuits.

Eating Disorders

There is more to food than meets the mouth. How you relate to food has a lot to do with your mental state. You may have noticed that many of the mental disorders tend to affect a person's relationship with food, either through overeating or not eating. Eating disorders can be manifested through an obsession with body weight, shape or food. For some people, the situation is so bad that they end up dead if the condition is not treated. Symptoms include food binges, severe food restriction, over-exercising or purging behaviors.

That is not all

There are many other mental illnesses, including different types of phobias and personality disorders. Some common and 'normal' emotions, like anger and loneliness, can easily turn into mental illnesses when they get out of hand and harm you or others. For instance, my father had anger issues that saw the death of my mother. In my anger, also, I wrecked my family, depriving them and myself of peace. At this point anger is no longer a natural emotion, but a mental problem that needs to be addressed.

Other behaviors, like hoarding, are not necessarily mental problems until they go to the extreme. They may also indicate the existence of another mental disorder.

Chapter Two

Safety Plan

When you are going through a mental illness, life can be tough and quite unbearable. Most days seem endless and full of pressure, while you lack the energy and the will to go through it. With negative thoughts and emotions weighing you down, it is expected that your behavior will align with how you feel and think. The result is guilt for behaving badly, hopelessness and a lack of motivation to get up.

I remember that Wednesday morning as I sat in my well-furnished executive office feeling empty and beaten. Despite the wealth and success, I felt like a failure and lost beyond redemption. At times like those, destructive thoughts creep in. You begin to feel that leaving this world is the only way to fill that hole within, quiet the constant buzz in the mind, and be accepted. While deadly thoughts keep showing up now and then, there are days when the cry for peace and quiet is so loud that it takes a lot of willpower to stop it. Without a safety plan, it is easy to answer this call and take the short and foolish route out. I know, I attempted it. I took those pills.

Since you are aware of the existence of such extra gloomy days, it is best to plan for them, and that is where the safety plan comes in. Diagnosis of a mental illness is not enough to keep you and others from harm. The safety plan will help you identify your red flags. You will know when you have started going downhill, and even the rate of acceleration, so you can seek the necessary help.

Even if you are not yet suicidal, as long as you have a mental disorder, it is best to have a safety plan. That way, you stay prepared in case things get out of hand. Knowing what to do takes away one more cause for anxiety.

Before you prepare your safety plan, you need to be at a good place. You can hardly think through your triggers when you are on the verge of self-harm. An appropriate time to prepare the plan is when you are recovering or stable. Have with you a mental-health provider and a family member or one of your support people. In case you are unable to realize the red flags, he can help you. Having someone to support you is also crucial, so you don't feel alone.

If you're wondering how having a safety plan helps your life, you can look at recent studies that show that it is an evidence-based intervention that reduces the risk of harming yourself or others. Patients who have a safety plan are less likely to self-harm than those without. Additionally, they tend to have subsequently better-quality engagements with the health-care providers. You should be part of the winning team, and a small step to take is the development of a safety plan.

The safety plan is your first aid kit to help you through a crisis and ensure that you stay safe before pulling the big guns, if necessary. It affords you time to calm down and feel more in control when those overwhelming thoughts come.

What to consider when developing a plan

When developing a safety plan, there are certain issues you need to consider to ensure that your plan works. You will realize that these vary from one individual to another, making it important for each person to develop a safety plan that is tailored to himself. Some of the questions you need to ask yourself include:

1. ***When to use the plan:*** You need to ask yourself at what point you need to use the plan. At this point, it is necessary to consider what triggers the deadly thoughts. Look at the possible situations, feelings or thoughts, and any warning signs that you can recognize. For example, if you stop eating when you're feeling depressed, then you know that is a sign to watch for.

2. ***How to comfort yourself:*** Similar to the above where you create a list of what sets you off on the dangerous path, here you also create a similar list but of those things that make you feel better so you can reduce the destructive thoughts. You need to look at things that make you feel protected and safe. For example, there are those who clean, or those for which food is the answer. For you, it might be taking a walk or listening to music. Whatever works for you, even if it is shouting or jumping up and down, do not hesitate to write it down.

3. ***Reasons for living:*** There are days so dark that you may not see any reason for being alive. All you want to do is disappear into thin air and

never feel pained or weighed down again. Before you get to that day, write down your reasons for living so that you remember why life is worth living. Your reasons could be anything like family, a pet, partner or anything else. There is no need to justify any of the reasons you choose. Even your potted plants, if they give you the joy and reason to live, then that's all that matters. You only need something or someone that makes life worth living.

4. ***Who to talk to:*** In our darkest hours, there are not many numbers on our phones that are worth dialing. In most cases, you hardly feel like talking to anyone. However, it is necessary that you find one or two people who you can talk to in those times. These are people who are not judgmental and who truly understand your situation and are willing to take the time to help you feel better. You can even ask them if you can add them to your list of people who you would reach out to when feeling down and having dangerous thoughts. Again, include people you feel comfortable talking to, like a friend, partner or even a priest.

5. ***Where to get professional help:*** In as much as it is important to have people around you, it is

also important to have a list of available and easily accessible professional help that can provide you with any support that you may need. The list can include mental-health professionals and helplines, email addresses and website addresses that you can reach out to.

6. ***How to make your environment safe:*** Sometimes all it takes is the presence of a potential weapon to push one over the edge. Therefore, you have to make a conscious decision to ensure that your environment is safe for you. You may need to secure items that you could use to harm yourself or even get out of an unsafe environment. You could also ask someone else to help you stay safe. For example, if you are likely to hurt yourself in the kitchen, it is best to get out of there. Alternatively, you may want to lock up any sharp items, like knives and pairs of scissors. Highly lethal methods or items, like firearms and poison, should not be left for the patient to restrict. A designated and responsible person, like a close friend, police or even a family member, should be charged with the responsibility of making these restrictions.

The questions above make up your safety plan. You need to document the answers and keep them in an easily accessible place for reference when you need them. The safety plan is best prepared with the input of a mental-health professional, as well as someone who you trust. You need all the help you can get, and it is always nice to have a team to discuss issues with, lest those issues overwhelm you. As you may have noted, making a safety plan is not rocket science, so you have nothing to worry about. The bulk of the work remains in ensuring that it is implemented.

What happens after developing the plan?

Alongside your mental-health-care team of professionals, it is important that you discuss the likelihood that the safety plan will be followed when the need arises. There is no need for taking time to develop a safety plan only for it to be discarded at the first sign of trouble. If you see any possible hindrances to the implementation of the safety plan, then this is a good time to disclose them for further discussion. Together, these concerns can be addressed to ensure that, when or if the time comes, you will follow the plan.

The safety plan has to be easily accessible to you at all times. After its development, it is also crucial that you discuss where you keep the plan, so it is safe yet easily accessible. You can have both a hard and soft copy that are placed in strategic places for your reference.

Another important factor is to evaluate if the format used for the plan is appropriate and fits within your capacity and circumstances. The idea is to keep the safety plan as simple as possible to avoid contradictions or any complicated phrases.

Finally, you have to keep reviewing the plan periodically to ensure that it is still effective. Over time, your circumstances are likely to change, and the plan needs to reflect this change. For example, if the person you reach out to when feeling overwhelmed moves to a different place and a different time zone, you may want to have someone else take their place and who can easily read you and the medical assistance that you need.

You need to note that sometimes having the safety plan is not enough to deter the dangerous feelings. If the feelings persist despite doing what your plan intends that you do, then it is time to ask for assistance from the nearest emergency room. Do not wait for tomorrow, and do not take yourself to the hospital. Instead, call the emergency services team for your area and request for transport to the hospital.

Implementing the Safety Plan

Now that you have a plan at hand, the next time you have such thoughts or signs of triggers that you recognize as red signs, take out your plan and follow the outlined course of action until you feel safe again. For example, if you are feeling unnaturally angry or very low, you can take a walk or use whatever way of calming yourself down that is in your plan until you feel better. However, if the feelings are very strong, you can simply call a trusted friend or emergency services who can come stay with you. If you can, take action at the onset of the thoughts or even when you recognize any red flags, so you are able to calm down sooner rather than later.

The safety plan is meant to be your support and, if, at any point, you feel overwhelmed, do not consider yourself a loser but be the champion by calling in emergency services. Remember, above all else, your life is most important.

Chapter Summary

Having a safety plan is a crucial step in the management of any mental illness.

- You have to know and recognize your triggers.
- Get a good support team.
- Be willing to follow the safety plan.
- Keep the plan updated as your recovery/illness progresses.

In the next chapter, you will learn about the first CBT technique that you can use to overcome anxiety, depression and intrusive thoughts: a technique called cognitive restructuring.

Chapter Three

Technique 1– Cognitive Restructuring

If we were all to be truthful, we would say that we have some days that are better than others. We all experience negative thoughts once in a while, but for some people, these thoughts become entrenched into them, almost becoming a part of them and thus interfering with their well-being, achievements and relationships. When you are in such a position, it becomes hard to think clearly and even more difficult to get those thoughts from your mind. You may be feeling beaten, but you are not done yet. The overwhelming and burdening thoughts that you have may seem to be taking center stage in your life, but there is a way of changing those thoughts.

What is Cognitive Restructuring?

Cognitive restructuring is a Cognitive Behavioral Therapy (CBT) technique, which helps you to notice as well as change those negative thinking patterns. Through cognitive restructuring, you can find ways to explore, interrupt and redirect self-defeating and destructive thoughts. The cognitive restructuring technique is known as a useful tool that can help you get a good understanding of those unhappy feelings, as well as for challenging the 'automatic beliefs' that are often wrong.

When beginning to use cognitive reconstructing, it is advisable to work with a therapist to help you overcome the hurdle of recognizing those faulty thought patterns that have made a home in your mind. Most times, you are so used to thinking in a particular way that it becomes very difficult to find those inaccuracies in your thought patterns that are causing you problems.

Cognitive restructuring has its foundation on cognitive mediation, which implies that your emotional feelings are not based on what happens to you but rather how you process and think about what happens to you. Here, it is literally the thought that counts. If you change how you think, you can also change how you feel.

Application and Success

Before we delve into how to carry out cognitive restructuring, you may want to know if it works or is a waste of time. Having been through the process, I can attest that this technique produces positive results. Over time, I have been able to successfully change those negative thinking patterns to positive ones, and I have seen my behavior and state of mind change for the better.

There are also many research studies that have shown that cognitive restructuring is an effective technique in the treatment of different conditions, such as depression, social phobias, PTSD, stress, anxiety, addictions and relationship issues. Furthermore, this technique has been proven to help people dealing with extreme grief.

You can easily apply cognitive restructuring into your everyday life when faced with those negative thoughts. However, do not pass up a chance to work through the process with a mental-health practitioner to ensure a higher chance of success.

Steps in Cognitive Restructuring

The cognitive restructuring framework is based on the Seven-Column Thought Record, designed by

Christine Padesky, and takes you through seven simple steps.

1. ***Calm down:*** Looking within yourself while stressed or upset is very difficult. The first step is to ensure that you are calm. You can take some time to engage in deep breathing or the use of meditation to calm yourself. Once calm, you can then begin the process and be able to deal with any intrusive thoughts.

2. ***Situation identification:*** The next step is to identify the situation you are in and what is triggering the negative mood. For example, is it something someone said to you? Was it a situation you walked into? The more specific you can be in this situation, the better. For instance, if you submit a report and someone makes a remark that sends you flying off the handle, think through the comment and pick out what exactly in that comment has destabilized your emotions.

3. ***Carry out mood analysis:*** Once you put a finger on the situation, you also need to analyze your mood through it. The key thing here is to focus and isolate the mood, while leaving out the thoughts. The easiest way to separate the two is to recognize that a thought tends to be complex.

For example, "He hated my report for including recommendations that he did not like." Moods are often easy to relate to and can be summarized in one word. For example, the incident resulted in humiliation, anger, sadness, frustration or insecurity.

4. ***Identify automatic thoughts:*** Next, you need to write down the automatic thoughts or the natural reactions that you experience when you feel the mood. For example, you may think you are stupid or that he is arrogant, or that you will never get that promotion, or that you were right. Whatever thought automatically crops into your mind after the mood kicks in, you need to write it down.

5. ***Find objectively supporting evidence:*** On this part, calmly and rationally look at a reason that supports why you are having those automatic thoughts. For example, the boss did not consider even one of my recommendations or even ask why I thought they were ideal." Here, your goal is to be as objective as possible while looking at the scenario, then write down the specific comment or event that caused you to have those automatic thoughts.

6. ***Find objectively contradicting evidence:*** Similar to the above, here you also look at the scenario objectively then identify and note down anything that evidently contradicts that automatic thought. For example, "Those recommendations were based on research findings." You can also look at your record and note that you have always produced quality reports and that you train new people on producing ideal reports. By looking at this and writing them down, you realize that these statements are fair and a true reflection of your position, as compared to the reactive thoughts.

7. ***Identify the thoughts that are fair and balanced:*** By now, you have carefully analyzed the situation and thought through your reactions. You have the necessary information to identify a fair and balanced perspective of the occurrences. However, you may still feel uncertain, so you can discuss the situation with another person or use another way to test the question. You can now write down the balanced thoughts. For example, you can note that your report contained the right information based on facts, and his way of handling the situation was not appropriate. Or you can write that, "I did my best on that report, and it was great except the

recommendations that the boss did not like." Do not look to justify yourself but to describe the situation as it is. If you realize there were errors on the report, acknowledge them but do not center on them. You can write that the report was wonderfully done but had a possibly misleading recommendation that did not alter the tone or the effectiveness of it.

8. ***Monitor your mood:*** Once you have calmly gone through the situation, you will realize that having a clear view makes you feel better. You are likely to be in a better mood feeling positive. Write down how you feel.

9. ***Reflect:*** Since you are already feeling better, it is a good time to reflect on what you can do about the situation. You may realize after writing down the fair and balanced view that you need not take any action and that it is not a big deal as you originally envisioned it. However, if you feel like there is something you can do, then go ahead. For example, if, after the comment, you got angry and banged the doors, you may want to go and apologize for that.

10. ***Create positive affirmations:*** There is power in our words. By making affirmations, you remind yourself of all the capabilities that you have and

convince yourself to embrace positivity. These positive utterances become part of you and will help to keep away any negative automatic thoughts in future.

The Challenge

The only challenge is that cognitive restructuring is not very easy to learn for some people. To put it into perspective, it is not difficult to learn either, but some people find identifying their moods and feelings and putting them into words to be difficult. Also, in the event that you make any thought errors, it is difficult to recognize them. Additionally, you may have trouble re-stating your thoughts in a way that does not make more thought errors.

The good news is that it is not all bleak. With patience, practice, and an open mind you can master cognitive restructuring. A helpful tactic is to have a third-party present during the process, preferably a therapist, who is able to critique your efforts while coaching you to succeed.

Why you should try cognitive restructuring

In addition to the high potential for success that comes with this technique, look at it as a type of mental weightlifting. The first time it is going to be challenging, and your muscles will ache just like what happens at the gym. However, you do not give up in those first days even as it seems extremely tough because your mental muscles are developing and strengthening. As you continually practice, it will get easier, and your mental muscles will gain strength. You will be surprised that, with time, they are so strong that you easily catch yourself when you start to have dysfunctional thinking and are able to correct the thought in real time, so you don't experience stress. Wouldn't you want that?

Today, I do not even consciously tell myself that I will undertake cognitive restructuring, it has become embedded in me and occurs almost automatically. Each time a negative and stress-inducing thought crops into my head, I am alert, and I calmly ask myself what caused it and correct my thought process. You can also experience the liberation that comes with not having to feel useless and weighed down.

Chapter Summary

In this chapter, we have looked at one CBT technique to address some of the major mental illnesses, including depression, anxiety and intrusive thoughts. We have learned that:

- Cognitive restructuring is a technique that focuses on identifying, challenging and altering the negative thoughts and making way for positive thoughts.
- Through this technique, you will learn to replace those rigid and hard-on-yourself thoughts with less rigid, more accurate and practical thoughts that align you to think positively.
- Although, initially the technique may be challenging, especially when it comes to being true to yourself and your thoughts, it gets better, easier and more effective as time goes on.
- Practice makes perfect.

In the next chapter, you will learn about another CBT technique on bursting mental distortions.

Chapter Four

Technique 2 – Bursting Mental Distortions

There are days when you wake up and feel like you are full of negativity. Some people believe that the day will be bad even before their feet touch the floor while others do not even have the will to get out of bed. The feeling is usually brought about something that your mind was focused on or a worry within you. True, we all do experience those negative feelings brought about by the negative thoughts we harbor.

You are not alone. Even those among us who take pride in being balanced thinkers are plagued with these negative thoughts from time to time. The difference is that they know when to burst such a thought and not allow it to grow roots. Psychologists call these inaccurate thoughts, which only work to reinforce negative emotions or thought patterns, cognitive distortions that make us interpret events in a negative light. Having cognitive distortions from time to time is normal. However, when they are reinforced, they deepen depression, increase anxiety, cause difficulties in relationships and result in other major complications.

Cognitive Distortions

You may wonder where these cognitive distortions come from and how best to deal with them. Evidence from research shows that people develop them as a means of coping with life's adverse events. The more severe and prolonged those events are, the stronger and more likely the cognitive distortions will be. Stress causes people to adapt their way of thinking in a way that is useful for their immediate survival. For example, if every time it gets dark it rains, people learn to prepare for rain at the first sight of darkness. Similarly, our early ancestors used cognitive distortions to adapt to the changing environment. However, as you may know, life is not constant and, while on a dark day it may rain, it is not given that every dark day brings rain with it. Therefore, constantly giving in to cognitive distortions results in habitual errors in thinking.

Let us look at some of the most common cognitive distortions that you are likely to be encouraging in your life. Sometimes we do not realize that we allow our thinking to be flawed by some of these distortions. More often than not, you may not even recognize them for what they are.

- ***Polarized Thinking:*** You can consider this to be 'all or nothing thinking.' Everything is either black or white without any room for gray or even the addition of color. It is either you are extremely good or a failure, and there is no middle ground. For example, you may think that you are a total failure if you do not play the piano well, even if you have just started playing. You're not recognizing that you are not skilled (yet) and need time to learn.

- ***Filtering:*** In this cognitive distortion, you may find that you ignore all the good and positive and instead focus all your attention and thoughts on the negative aspect albeit however small it may be. For example, if you invite people over for dinner and everyone comes except for one person, you spend the evening focused on why he didn't come and allowing negative thoughts to cloud your mind instead of enjoying dinner with the company that is attending.

- ***Jumping to conclusions:*** Here, you find yourself drawing conclusions and being sure of something even without any evidence. For example, you may conclude that the one person who did not attend your dinner does not like you and that the one who did attend only came to mock you. Also, you may find yourself believing that whatever fears you have will come true even before you have the chance to find out.

- ***Overgeneralization:*** We all tend to overgeneralize from time to time. Overgeneralization involves taking a single and isolated incident and drawing broad conclusions from it. For example, if you fail one job interview, you may conclude that you are terrible at interviews and may never get a job.

- ***Personalization:*** There are people who carry the weight of the world on their shoulders simply by personalizing matters. They feel like their actions impact other people or external events and, hence, hold themselves responsible. For example, they may feel like by buying the last container of milk at the store they are the reason it has run out and others will not have any.

- *Magnifying, Minimizing or Catastrophizing:* There are two sides to this: either minimizing the positives or magnifying the negatives. In this distortion, the person may take a small mistake made and catastrophize it. For example, if she is late for a meeting, she may think that the entire project will run late because of it and worry about being fired for derailing the project. On the other hand, she may play down any accomplishment she achieves and reduce herself to mere invisibility.

- *Control fallacies:* Some of us like being in control of everything and that everything that happens to us is either out of our own actions or purely external forces. People with control fallacies have a hard time accepting that sometimes things happen from forces that we can't control. For example, a person with this cognitive distortion will assume that other people's performances are not good because of them, or theirs is not good because of a difficult co-worker.

- *Blaming:* Most often, when things go wrong, we have to find a way of explaining the outcome. Some people opt to blame others for making them feel or act in a certain manner, which is a cognitive distortion. No matter how someone contributes to the situation, the only person solely responsible for how you act or feel is you.

- ***Fairness fallacies:*** As a matter of fact, life is not fair. However, there are people who go through life so fixated on fairness that they end up unhappy and resentful when they do not get it.

- ***Emotional reasoning:*** If you are one of those people who has a strong false belief in your emotions, then that is a cognitive distortion. The way you feel about a situation cannot be necessarily true and, hence, is not a definite or accurate indicator of reality. Listening to, validating and expressing emotions is important, but you should judge things based on reality and rational evidence.

- ***Labeling:*** There are people who reduce themselves or others to a single, mainly negative, descriptor or characteristic, such as a failure or being stupid. Labeling causes people to criticize themselves and also causes the thinker to either underestimate or misunderstand others due to the misperception.

- **Positive discounting:** Similar to filtering, people who discount the positive have a negative bias in their thinking. They tend to explain any positive away as a fluke or luck instead of acknowledging that good things do occur as a result of skills, determination and smart choices.

- **The 'should' people:** Have you met one of those people who always has a list of what should be done or said in a certain situation? He should be able to do this when that happens. His thinking is limited to this and will usually have a negative perspective of life. Most of these kinds of people are rooted in internalized cultural or family expectations that are not appropriate as they tend to increase anxiety and reduce self-esteem.

How to Burst Cognitive Distortions

In this section, we look at what you can do to fix those irrational and automatic thoughts, as well as cognitive distortions.

1. Identify it

The first step is to identify the kind of distortion that you are harboring and its extent in your life. This is similar to when you get sick and the doctor examines you to determine the problem and, thus, the solution. You can only work to change what you know to be the problem. Start by tracking your thoughts daily and identifying any cognitive distortions. A simple way of doing this is by developing a list of troublesome thoughts as they keep coming, then you can comb through them and see if they match up with any cognitive distortions.

Taking time to go through your negative and intrusive thoughts at a later time helps you to realize what cognitive distortion(s) you are leaning toward. You can also take this opportunity to carefully look into each problem in a calm, realistic and natural manner. Consider it as keeping a mood log.

2. Examine the evidence

Here, you need to distance yourself from the emotionality of the upsetting episode or event, then take the judge's seat to examine the evidence objectively. You will be able to identify the basis for your distorted view.

You can easily achieve this by looking at individual thoughts linked to an event, and then objectively deciding whether they are a reflection of either a fact or an opinion. For example, thoughts such as, "I am stupid" or "I am selfish" are opinions. On the other hand, statements like, "My boss spoke to me angrily" or "I submitted the report late" are facts. You need to separate the facts and opinions so you can determine which is a cognitive distortion, then you can work on that.

3. Apply the double-standard method

As an alternative to the negative, demeaning and harsh self-talk that you keep telling yourself, consider turning this negative talk into a caring and compassionate one, such as one you would give a friend. Most people with mental illnesses tend to be very hard on themselves while being more accommodating to friends and relatives.

You should take the time to go through your thoughts and situation, look at yourself as a close friend and have a similar conversation as you would have with her, heck, even make that important cup of tea, and converse. Would you tell your friends after working hard on a report that she was going to screw up, and it wasn't any good? Chances are high that you would tell them not to worry because they did give it their best and that the report was going to be exceptionally well-received. Tell yourself the same thing, be your own friend. Besides, in a world with few friends, it helps to have one within.

4. Welcome the shades of gray

When you are carrying different cognitive distortions, your mind tends to simplify the processing of stimuli and will often rush to make a decision or choose a response. Although black and white thinking or polarized thinking do serve a good purpose of hastening decision-making and responses, it can also take you on a road of irrational belief. You need to welcome the shades of gray and stop focusing on either black or white.

When the plan did not fully succeed, don't look at it as having failed but instead evaluate it on a scale of 0 and 100. That way, you get to appreciate the amount that is achieved, and also understand how much is remaining and why. For example, if you have been working hard at something then get so tired you take a day off, don't think the effort of the days worked is wasted because of that one day. If you decide to work out and have been doing so for weeks, then one day you don't work out and have that cake, don't give up because you think you are a failure. Look at the scale and appreciate how much you have gotten done, then analyze and see that the one day of being easy on yourself could be beneficial to re-energize you. The overall likelihood of ruining everything could be around two percent, a very negligible number.

5. Experiment

Another way of bursting cognitive distortions is to experiment, much like scientists do when trying to prove a hypothesis. The idea here is to look for evidence that those thoughts you are having are true.

For example, if you have been thinking that you are unable to do a certain task and so, as a result, you have neglected to even attempt it. You could test that perceived inability by breaking the task into small subtasks and attempting to do just one or two. You may be surprised that you can make a lot of progress and that will prove that your thought on it was a cognitive distortion. For example, if you have been telling yourself that you are not good enough and cannot pass that class, start by registering for it and attending the first class with an open mind. You may realize that you enjoy the content and end up doing really well.

Take time to test those thoughts; do not allow them to intimidate you. If you think your friends hate you, ask them to dinner, and you may be surprised to see how glad they are that you reached out. Develop a policy that says that it is not true until proven so. You will note that the cognitive distortions will begin to disappear as they know they are bound to be proven wrong.

6. Take a survey

When you feel weighed down, in doubt and filled with negative intrusive thoughts, it helps to talk to someone. They say a problem shared is half-solved. In this case, go a little further and ask people their opinions on the reality of your attitude and thoughts. Preferably, ask people who are in a similar situation to yours.

For example, if you are working hard on your body through exercise and eating healthy and believe that falling into the temptation of a cheat meal is unforgivable, you can ask your gym instructor or that well-toned girl. They will tell you that cheating on your meals happens every so often, and it is nothing to fret over as long as you don't make it a habit. You can even double-check by asking the same question to a few more people to hear their experiences.

7. Watch the semantics

If you are one of the people stuck in the world of 'should' or 'should not', it is time to get out of it. Using 'should' statements applies unwritten rules to how you can behave, which is something that may not make any sense to others. 'Should' statements imply that you are judging your behavior or that of another person, which is hurtful and unnecessary.

When you catch yourself starting to make a should statement, try something else like, "It would be good or nice if…". That creates a more positive feel. For instance, you could say, "It would be nice if I started exercising for better health." The positivity of the statement first gives you a choice, hence, making you feel in control and increasing your chances of taking up exercise. At the same time, if, for some reason, you cannot exercise, maybe due to health concerns, it still gives you a way out without feeling like a failure.

In a similar situation, if you use should, you end up feeling as though you ought to and if you don't or cannot for whatever reason, you have failed, which is not true. You can take back control by simply changing your semantics.

8. Look up the definition

Yes, I mean get a dictionary or go to the Internet and search the meaning of those labels that you are giving to yourself and others. This method works better for the intellectual people who like to argue on the basis of facts, but can work with anyone who is willing to look up the meaning of words and phrases. Once you are armed with information, you can argue against your cognitive distortions.

If you have labeled yourself as stupid or inferior, looking at the meaning of the words will instantly tell you that these labels do not refer to a person in his entirety but rather to specific behaviors. You can then go on to ask further questions like, "Stupid in what? Have I been taught or trained? For how long? How much do I know? Stupid compared to who? How much does the other person know? What level of education and experience does he have?" As you think about the definitions, you delve further into questioning your reasoning and realize that such labels are not true and are a waste of your brain power.

9. Re-attributions

Some of us suffer from blaming and from personalized cognitive disorders, meaning that they point at themselves and take the fall for every negative thing that they experience. They believe that they are synonymous with causing bad things. If you are one of these people, you do not look at the actual cause but rather convince yourself that it is because of you.

Re-attribution helps you to identify external factors or people that contribute to the event or problem, so you stop blaming yourself. By assigning responsibility where it is due, you are not deflecting blame but rather showing the true contributors and not placing the entire blame on you. You will then have the energy not to feel bad for causing something you did not cause, but to pursue resolutions to the problems and find ways of dealing with the predicaments. For example, if you are a six-person team working on a research project, and the work is not done in due time due to adverse weather that prevents field work from going on as planned, you cannot blame yourself for the delay. You have to acknowledge the role of nature and then split the responsibility among the six of you, making it ⅙th your responsibility. Instead of wallowing in guilt for missed deadlines, you should be working to find a way to fast-track the remaining work.

10. Weigh the costs and the benefits

In this method of bursting cognitive distortions, you rely on motivation rather than facts. Here, you list the pros and cons of thoughts, feelings and behaviors that you are experiencing. You can, therefore, figure out what you are gaining by having that distorted thinking, feeling bad and behavior that is inappropriate.

You will have to look within and ask yourself how believing and holding on to the situations and negative thinking helps you. If, after listing the pros and cons, you find that the cons outweigh the pros, then you are better off without the distortions and irrational thinking. You have the weapon to talk back those ugly thoughts and welcome the positive ones.

How to Stop or Slow Down Cognitive Distortions

Now that you know how to burst those cognitive distortions, it is also important to know how to slow down or stop those distortions when they creep up. In addition to finding the right way to unravel those distortions, here is a simple way of stopping them, or at least slowing them down, when they occur.

- ***Identify and isolate that intrusive or negative thought:*** Examine your thoughts well and recognize some words that are clues to cognitive distortions, such as 'never', 'always' or 'can't'. Other strong and negative words, such as loser, foolish or hate should also give you clues into cognitive distortions.

- ***Write it down:*** By now, you may realize the importance of writing things down. Writing down those thoughts make them come alive so you can assess them easily.

- ***Check your distress temperature:*** On a scale of 0 to 10, with zero being peaceful and content and 10 being the feeling of the whole world ending, check where you fall on that scale.

- ***Is it reasonable?*** The next question to ask is if the thought you are having is reasonable. Be very honest with yourself and answer if you think your thinking pattern makes sense. An easy way of doing so is saying the thought out loud. For example, "I am stupid." Assume a friend or colleague said that to you. Would you agree? If you find that the thought you are having is reasonable, there is a likelihood that it is not a cognitive distortion. For instance, if you think you are lazy and you find that it is true, then take stock of what caused the thought, then decide to do something about it, or let go or even let go of the thought but work on the cause. There is always much good to be gained by taking responsibility. If you haven't been finishing your tasks, create a program to ensure you get them done in good time. You will feel good about it and reduce the weight of such a thought.

- ***If unreasonable, figure out the distortion:*** On the other hand, if the thought is unreasonable, pin it down to the type of distortion it is so you can use the means discussed above to burst it. Usually, people have a tendency to have a certain pattern. You could be having fairness fallacies or mental filtering, among others. Identify what pattern you are displaying, then work on overcoming the distortion.

- ***Develop a reasonable thought:*** Having identified that you have cognitive distortions and that your thoughts are unreasonable, it is time to come up with a more reasonable thought to take the place of the distorted one. For example, instead of saying you are stupid, you can acknowledge that you are semi-skilled in data analysis and could use more training in the field. Remember to write it down to give it life and permanence. If you cannot think of anything, think about what a friend would say.

- ***Recheck that distress temperature:*** Check your level of distress again to see if it had dropped by a few levels. Appreciate even the slightest drop as it signifies that you are moving in the right direction.

- ***Practice:*** Similar to cognitive restructuring, gaining a hold of your thoughts is not an easy exercise. You will be required to keep practicing and teaching yourself to think positive thoughts until it becomes natural for you. There is hope. You can do it. Over time and with commitment, you can burst those cognitive distortions that threaten your peace and happiness.

Chapter Summary

In this chapter, we have learned about cognitive distortions, bursting them and how to slow down their intrusion.

- Cognitive distortions refer to repeated ways of thinking that often are negative and inaccurate.
- Some of the most common cognitive distortions include mental filtering, overgeneralization, polarized thinking, catastrophizing, personalization, emotional reasoning, labeling and 'should' statements.
- You can break away from cognitive distortions by using methods, such as cost-benefit analysis, definition, experiments, use of semantics and re-attribution, among others.
- The key to breaking from cognitive distortions is identifying the issue, and then going on to find its rationality. In many cases, you will realize that the thoughts are incorrect and irrational.
- Always replace the irrational thought with a more accurate and rational thought.

In the next chapter, you will learn about journaling and the benefits that come with putting things down in writing, as well as how it helps to improve your mental health.

Chapter Five

Technique 3 – Write it Down

———— ◆ ◇ ◆ ————

By now, you have realized that we are constantly talking about the need to write down the thoughts. You may be thinking that these thoughts occur all the time, and you have no time to keep writing them down. As inconveniencing as it sounds, it is good practice to note down those thoughts as they occur. Doing so later will mean that you will struggle to understand your mood at that time and remember the particular thoughts and meaning. When you catch them raw, you are in a better place to articulate them and put down the feelings as they occur.

Think back to when you were younger, a pre-teen, teen or even a young adult. Chances are high that you kept a diary hidden under your bed. In it were your innermost thoughts, challenges and experiences. You wrote down the thoughts that mattered and those that you could not share with another person. You knew you could trust the diary to be part of your thoughts without any judgement. You were free to write down any thoughts. and the diary absorbed them, making you feel lighter yet protected.

As you grew older, you probably stopped keeping a diary and thoughts began crashing into you. The weight that the diary took has not found another home and so is held within you. While you may have friends and family that you can talk to, sometimes you may have deep thoughts that you would rather not share. Writing down your experiences, thoughts and moods makes them not only clearer but also helps you gain control of them and benefits your mental health.

What does writing it down mean?

Also known as journaling, it is a practice of writing down thoughts and events to meet your set goals and improve the quality of life. Each person has a unique way of writing things down and a particular reason, but the outcome has been mostly positive. You may have heard someone ask you about your dreams and goals, and then inquire if you had them written down. By writing them down, you can reach your goals because you are clear on what you want to achieve and can craft a way of how to do just that. Journaling helps in clearing your mind, connecting thoughts, feelings, and behaviors, as well as buffering or reducing effects of mental disorders.

How does it work?

Writing your thoughts and feelings down uses the rational and analytical left side of the brain, giving space and room for the touchy-feely and creative right side to be free to play and wander. The effect is that your creativity flourishes, expanding the cathartic and making a positive impact on your well-being.

Benefits of journaling for mental health

There are many benefits you get from developing a habit of expressive writing. Some of them include:

- Managing anxiety
- Coping with depression
- Stress reduction
- Helping in the prioritization of fears, concerns and problems
- Daily tracking of symptoms to recognize triggers and learn coping and control strategies
- Identification of negative behaviors and thoughts

- Provision of opportunities for positive self-talk
- Improving your working memory
- Reducing intrusive thoughts and avoidance symptoms
- Boosting your mood
- Enhancing a sense of well-being
- Clearing and calming the mind
- Opening your mind to your successes and struggles
- Tracking your mental-health progress
- Acts as a release for pent-up feelings
- Helps to enhance self-awareness
- Helps in considering multiple options and planning

Writing down our thoughts enhances your mental health by guiding you to confront emotions that were previously inhibited, thus reducing the stress that comes with the inhibitions. Further, it helps you to process difficult events. For example, if you are grieving the loss of a loved one, writing it down helps you open up about how terrible it feels and to process the event. You also have the opportunity to develop a coherent narrative about the event and your experiences and, hence, you can deal with its trauma. Having this time to intimately deal with your emotions is crucial to healing.

In case you are facing a traumatic experience, writing it down enhances your mental health by making you more self-aware. You can also easily detect unhealthy thinking and behavioral patterns that may be sneaking in, which, in turn, allows you to have more control so you can put things in order before it is late.

An additional benefit of journaling is that it helps you embrace a positive mindset and move from a negative one, since you are aware of what is going on within you. In essence, it strengthens your cognitive functioning.

Tips for constructive journaling

For you to harness the benefits that come with journaling, it has to be done effectively. While you may choose to dump words on a page, you may feel better, but you will certainly miss out on all the other amazing benefits, such as reduced stress, intrusive thoughts, anxiety and depression. Here are some tips you can follow when writing down your thoughts for mental health:

   a) *Have some private space:* You are about to note down some of your most private and intimate thoughts, and you certainly do not need people craning their necks to read them. Find a personalized space that does not have distractions.

b) ***Make it a habit:*** When starting out, you can write down your thoughts three to four times a week but work on increasing that to every day. If possible, write down when an intrusive thought occurs. There are now smartphone applications that you can use for this purpose, so you don't need a pen and paper.

c) ***Take time to reflect:*** After writing, take time to go through what you wrote quietly and objectively so you can balance yourself. Sometimes you do not even have to think about what you wrote but try to relax and balance your thoughts, particularly, when the thoughts are quite heavy.

d) ***No need to be specific:*** As much as it would be best to capture each thought and place it within an event, you do not have to do that. If you are working to overcome trauma, you do not have to write the specific event that caused the trauma. All you have to do is write about what you feel at that moment and what feels right to be written.

e) ***Structure as you please:*** The focal point of journaling is to get your thoughts and moods out of you and onto a page. There is no set structure or formula on how to do that. Write it however you feel is best.

f) ***Ensure it's private:*** Make sure to keep your journal private and away from unwanted eyes and hands. Knowing that it is safe makes you feel safe, too, and encourages you to keep writing. If you have to share or discuss it, then you can do so with your therapist.

WRITE Guidelines

A set of guidelines that has been useful for me in this journey are the WRITE guidelines, as they are simple to remember and effective in journaling. All you have to keep in mind is WRITE.

- *W stands for What to write about.* There are no restrictions on What to write, but some people find it difficult to write anything down and end up staring at a blank page for hours. Write about your current feelings, thoughts and anything and everything that is going on in your life. You can even write about your goals and what you are striving to achieve.

- *R stands for Review.* Writing is not enough to get you to understand your inner thoughts. Take some time to Review as well as Reflect on what you are writing. You need to be calm, still, collected and focused for this step. If you are feeling unsettled, you can opt for a little meditation or mindfulness. It is best to use 'I' statements, such as "I feel..." or "I think...". Try also to keep your writing in the present, for example, "Today I have been in a foul mood." "Now I feel..."

- **I stands for Investigate.** You need to investigate your feelings and thoughts as you write. Sometimes the mind may start wandering around instead of staying focused, especially if you are running out of things to write. In such instances, take time to go through what you have written and add any thoughts or events you may have left out. Alternatively, you can take time for re-focusing through meditation or mindfulness. Once you feel ready, keep writing.

- **T stands for Time.** Have a goal for how much time you want to spend writing on the minimum. Initially, even a minute may seem a lot, but set a goal and work toward it. For example, you can choose to spend at least five minutes each day writing. Note down the time as you begin to write alongside the projected end time. You can set an alarm to keep you aware of the time. Over time, as you get used to writing, you will begin to enjoy how therapeutic it is, and you will look forward to the activity.

- ***E stands for Exit.*** After writing, do not dump your journal and bail out until the next time. No, you need to exit strategically and with a level of soul-searching. Go through what you have written and reflect on it. Sum up what you have read as a conclusion to your thoughts and an observation. For example, you can note that, "As I read this, I note that I have been focusing only on the negative side of life." You can also take this opportunity to come up with action points for you to commit to. For example, "I will be intentional in drawing out the positive things that happen." Also write your action items down so you can follow through.

Be You, Do You

Many people take up journaling for different reasons. Some write for fun, others for work, while many people find that it provides an avenue to express themselves. When you are writing for your mental health, it is important that you focus on the objective of getting better, but do not allow it to be a source of unnecessary pressure.

As with everything else, the beginning is bound to be challenging. You may find that you do not know what to write. Now is not the time to worry about it but to get you started. Write about anything; how you feel, what your thoughts are and even events that happened. As you mature into it, you will learn to focus your writing on relevant thoughts and reflect on them. You will even go further to analyze and realize where you went wrong and work on correcting that. The idea is to start writing.

Do not aim for perfection; aim for self-expression. Ensure that you are honest with yourself and are able to look deep within you and articulate your feelings and thoughts. Over time, refine the process as per the guidelines, and you will witness the power of writing.

I remember my first days of writing were particularly hard because I had never kept a diary, even as a teenager. However, I have learned to enjoy writing down my thoughts and feelings. I consider it as having a second non-judgmental me to go through my day with me, combing through my deepest thoughts and reflecting on the struggles and successes. When I am overcome with thoughts that I cannot share with others, I am happy to know that I have somewhere I can pour them and not have to worry about consequences. I come out feeling lighter and happier.

Chapter Summary

In this chapter, we have looked at journaling, the associated benefits of writing down your thoughts and feelings and the best way to do it. In summary:

- Effective journaling involves writing down your thoughts and feelings, as well as experiences, and taking time to reflect on them.
- Journaling has numerous benefits, including providing an avenue to release pent-up emotions, managing anxiety, prioritization of fears and concerns, and opportunities for positive self-talk that breaks negative thoughts.
- You can apply the WRITE guideline in journaling that calls for knowing What to write, Reflecting, Investigating, Time and Exiting strategically.
- At the end of the day, write as you want first before building in the reflecting and going forward.
- Start today and keep growing. Practice makes perfect.

In the next chapter, you will learn about another useful CBT technique: exposure and response prevention.

Chapter Six

Technique 4 – Exposure and Response Prevention

You may not welcome the idea of exposing yourself to the same things that trigger anxiety and obsessions or send you into a full panic attack. Don't run off yet, hear me out. Exposing yourself to the triggers and them being beneficial is what exposure and response prevention is all about. My initial encounter with this CBT technique had me all packed up and wearing my running shoes. There was no way I was going to put myself through that. You probably have the same thought, but take some time and let's explore how this can help you heal and find peace.

In Exposure and Response Prevention (ERP), the Exposure aspect means that you expose yourself to objects, images, situations and thoughts that ruffle your feathers, making you nervous, anxious and bringing up all your obsessions. The second part of ERP, the Response Prevention, calls for you to not give in to all that ruffling and try to remain calm even after all the triggers are on. I know all this sounds scary, bearing in mind how our triggers bring out the worst in us.

You can think of those triggers as alarm bells. Once an alarm goes off, it calls for your attention and tells you it is time to spring into action. For instance, if, when you are sleeping and your security alarm system goes off, you know there is an intruder and to call the police even if it's the cat that set it off. No matter what sets off the alarm, we respond in a similar way, seeking to protect us and our families.

Similarly, these triggers are supposed to get your attention, more like a warning and for you to get ready to deal with whatever is coming. However, with mental illnesses, the triggers sound like danger to us and make us react in a compulsive way. You do not even get time to investigate if it is a real break-in or a bat that landed on the window triggering the alarm system. Often, we allow any trigger, even the minute ones, to sound like seven gunmen broke down the door with guns blaring.

Most of the time, those triggers you allow to hold you captive are negligible, yet you make them sound like a catastrophic and terrifying threat. You may find that, when the alarm goes off, it communicates danger instead of asking you to pay attention to the fact that there could be potential danger.

Understandably, it may be difficult to make a decision on starting the ERP technique, as it feels like you are deliberately exposing yourself to danger. However, through ERP, you will be able to change your brain functioning. Have you realized that most of the time that you feel like you are in danger you actually know that you are not? In those moments, you are unable to control your reactions and end up thinking the worst and behaving similarly. Starting on the ERP journey will help you take control of your thoughts and emotions and consequently your behavior. The beginning is bound to be challenging, so it is best to start off with a qualified therapist. After a while, you will find it easy to undertake ERP by yourself.

Is it Effective?

Before you put yourself through what appears to be torture, although I assure you it isn't, you may be interested to know if it is worth it. Yes, it is worth the effort.

There are many studies that have found ERP to be effective, particularly in the long-term treatment of OCD and anxiety. Unlike medication, where the symptoms tend to return after the dosage wears off, the effects of the success of ERP lasts beyond the treatment. Besides, the Emotional Processing Theory asserts that there are powerful lessons involved in the ERP treatment method.

How does it work?

The mechanism by which ERP works is best explained by two cognitive models: the inhibitory-learning model and habituation-learning model.

People mainly develop disorders from misinterpreting the significance of normally occurring intrusive thoughts that we all experience at different points in life. Furthermore, having dysfunctional thoughts, such as overestimation of threat, search for perfectionism, a need to control thoughts and an inflated sense of responsibility for the protection of self and others, all fuel OCD by making you interpret intrusive thoughts as significant and dangerous.

ERP helps to disconfirm those distorted beliefs by exposing you to the stimuli. If you have an intense fear of crossing roads as you expect to be knocked down, then repeatedly having to cross a road and subsequently *not* getting knocked down will alleviate that fear. Additionally, ERP also breaks the conditioned response that you have between obsessions and compulsions.

Habituation-Learning Model

Habituation is the reduction of fearful emotions and anxious psychological responses to frequent stimuli. The habituation-learning model works by causing a shift in the patient's belief system, such as overestimation of the risk associated, and by causing a reduction in the link between the threat appraisal and the belief.

Naturally, we tend to respond to stimuli through the fight-or-flight response. However, during ERP, you realize that the sympathetic nervous system that is responsible for anxiety's physiological part cannot indefinitely maintain the fight-or-flight response. In habituation, after some exposure time, approximately an hour after exposure, the parasympathetic nervous system gets triggered to help in settling down its sympathetic counterpart. The process happens regardless of how you cognitively interpret the situation. You therefore have to correct the cognitive schemas, even in the face of a feared stimulus in order to achieve homeostasis.

Habituation means that you have to change your behavior first so that the cognitions are modified then the emotions also change. In simple language, habituation calls for you to feed corrective information into your mind so that the body can settle down, your behavior can normalize and then your emotions become stable.

For example, if you are afraid of dirt and germs and associate them with the ability to contract a deadly incurable illness, then you will find that you avoid touching certain things, such as the trash can, public washroom handles, sinks and other highly contaminated areas. During the event, you don't keep washing your hands over and over again. In habituation, the therapist will expose you to those surfaces that you dread touching and make you touch them. You may be asked to touch the sink, the trash can and the washroom door handle; that is Exposure. Even as you feel like your world is exploding with germs, the therapist might then ask you to join her for a meal without allowing you to wash your hands even once, let alone seven times. Having a meal with unscrubbed hands may prove to be the real test, as you can imagine all the germs crawling on you. Here, that is the Response Prevention.

Initially, you will realize, as you touch those seemingly dirty surfaces, that your anxiety levels are likely to spike, but will begin to stabilize the more you touch the surfaces. After eating a meal and not immediately falling sick, you will also realize that the fear is exaggerated. You will then modify your earlier thinking and lessen the likelihood of contracting deadly diseases from dirty surfaces. You will become more accommodating of dirt than before, as you have seen that nothing much happened. Repeated exposure to the stimuli may even dissipate the fear.

Inhibitory-Learning Model

The inhibitory-learning model of ERP, unlike habituation, proposes that the association between the obsession/stimuli and the fear continues to exist and the links do not break. Instead, exposure to the stimuli brings in safety-based and new inhibitory associations. The model aims to ensure that patients learn that, at times, their feared outcomes occur when exposed to the stimulus, but other times the outcome they so fear does not occur. Thus, they have to develop both cognitive and emotional flexibility to prepare and deal with whatever outcome.

In essence, you learn to be more tolerant toward distress as well as being in contact with what is presently happening, rather than sitting back and waiting for the homeostasis process to kick in, as in habituation. Here, you do not sit back and wait for nature to take its course but rather are prepared for the possibility of your fears coming alive or not. You react to the immediate situation and what is happening, rather than freeze and wait for the body to try and stabilize. You invest in the present rather than in a would-be outcome.

The inhibitory-learning model helps you build adaptiveness by shifting focus from possible future-oriented outcomes to the present experiences and values. Besides, it gives you power and control by putting you in charge. You learn that the choice to decide on where to place your focus is in your hands. You can focus on what is happening presently or the future possibilities without necessarily having to wait for habituation to occur. You make the decision on where to place your thoughts and energy, which is empowering.

Conducting ERP

You may want to conduct your initial ERP with a therapist. However, there is no limit to the number of places that it can be done. Depending on the intensity level of the illness, ERP can be in an outpatient or residential treatment setting, partial hospitalization or even at home. Whatever your intensity level, there are some elements that form part of the ERP process.

- **Assessment and Planning for Treatment:** The clinician or a relevant health-care provider carries out assessment and provides you with psychoeducation. You learn about the available treatment methods and discuss your symptoms.

- **Trigger identification:** You work alongside your therapist to identify external objects, people and situations that trigger anxiety and obsessive thoughts. You also look internally into your physiological reactions and thoughts to see which ones cause distress and obsessive behavior.

- **Specify the content of obsessions and compulsions:** At this point, you also discuss how the two functionally relate, as well as identify the feared outcome, such as dying or contracting an illness. If you like to wash your hands 10 times, you may have a fear of getting infected if you do not, or you simply feel disgusted by dirt on your hands and will keep washing until when you feel clean.

- **Rank situations:** Together, rank the situations from the least distressing to the most distressing, based on your level of fear.

- **Coaching:** Having established a good background, it is time for you to undergo coaching by being exposed to situations or objects on your fear hierarchy while you work at not engaging in compulsions. You may also be exposed to imaginary situations where you envision your feared outcomes.

- **Learning to cope:** As you go through the exposure, you begin to realize that, in most cases, the worst scenario (in your head) does not occur. You do not fall ill after touching the dirty surface nor does that imaginary situation lead to the perceived consequences.

- **Post-exposure processing:** After each session, you will review the experiences, the violation of the expectations and the lessons learned.

- **Homework:** In most cases, the therapist will ask you to continually practice exposures on your own as you learned to eliminate daily rituals. You will realize that over time you begin to move up your fear hierarchy and are able to literally face most of them and easily confront distressing situations.

I do understand that literally facing your fears may not be something that you are willing to try. However, it is a great way to address them head on. Besides, I will tell you that it sounds harder than it actually is. Touching the first dirty surface is harder than touching the fifth one because, by then, your distress will be lower.

Having not to respond is what I found more challenging, but you learn and realize that you can actually go through life without the unnecessary compulsions. The more you are exposed to the stimuli, the lesser the distress level until you get to the point where it falls on the lower side of your fear hierarchy.

As earlier mentioned, you may want to start ERP with a therapist for encouragement before venturing out on your own. Things get easier with each exposure, and the burden is lifted. You will enjoy life without the obsessions and compulsions.

Chapter Summary

In this chapter, we have learned about the ERP method of mastering your brain and overcoming anxiety and OCD. In particular, we have learned that:

- ERP stands for Exposure and Response Prevention.
- By being exposed to the stimuli that trigger anxiety and OCD, you learn to prevent response and therefore gain control.
- You can use either the habituation- or inhibitory-learning models.
- Habituation calls for your mind to be exposed to the trigger until it automatically begins homeostasis while in the inhibitory-learning model, you learn that you have choices. You can either take what is presently happening or expect the worst possible outcome.
- It is advisable that you start ERP with a therapist before attempting it on your own. Initially, it can be intimidating for many people to face their triggers.

In the next chapter, you will learn another CBT technique that calls for you to relax. While it sounds like a simple task for ordinary people, it can be pretty difficult for anyone battling any mental illness. There is the yearning to be able to relax. Let us learn how to do so.

Chapter Seven

Technique 5 – Relax

You are probably thinking that it is easier said than done. When battling mental illnesses, particularly anxiety, depression and intrusive thoughts, you may find it difficult to relax. There are 10s of things wrong and 1,000 more that could potentially go wrong. You are likely always in a state of turmoil, fighting one thing or another, and it is tiring. The good news is that you can relax! Yes, even you are entitled to relaxation; it is not for the chosen few.

When faced with stressful situations, we tend to respond using the stress response, which comes naturally to help us survive like in prehistoric times when our ancestors had to employ the stress response to live through floods or even animal attacks. Despite the change in lifestyle over the years, we still face threatening situations that set off our stress responses. I am certain you can name several occasions when you feel the familiar pounding of the heart, increased breathing and the tension fill the muscles. At such times, relaxation is the last thing on your mind.

Since it is not possible to do away with all the stressors in life, it is important to learn how to activate the relaxation response. The relaxation response technique was first developed at Harvard Medical School in the 1970s by Dr. Herbert Benson, who was a cardiologist. The stress response is the opposite of the relaxation response. The relaxation response denotes profound rest. It may sound like a dream now, but with regular practice you can make a relaxed well of calm that you can tap into whenever necessary.

Relaxation Techniques

There are various relaxation techniques in CBT that you can learn. The key is to find what works well for you. Let us explore some of the techniques you can add to your daily routine to help you relax.

1. Breathing techniques

Did you know that there are several ways that you can breathe to reduce anxiety and stress, improve your lungs and help you to relax? To add breathing exercises to your daily life, you must make time for it. As little as two to five minutes a day are enough to make a difference. You can practice several times a day to get the best out of these breathing exercises. Some of the exercises include:

- *Pursed lip breathing:* Here, the aim is to slow down your breathing by ensuring that you apply deliberate effort. All you have to do is relax both the neck and shoulders, then with the mouth closed, gently inhale through the nose for two counts. Purse or pucker the lips as if whistling, then slowly exhale by blowing the air through the puckered lips for four counts.

- *Diaphragmatic breathing:* If you need to need to seriously relax and feel rested, all you have to do is practice diaphragmatic breathing for about five to 10 minutes a day. You need to lie down on your back with your head on a pillow and knees bent slightly. Take one hand and place it below your ribcage while the other goes on your upper chest so you can feel the diaphragm move. Gently inhale through the nose, so you feel the stomach press into the hand while keeping the other hand as still as possible. Exhale through pursed lips keeping your upper hand still and tightening your stomach muscle. To make it more difficult, you can put a book on your abdomen. Once you learn to belly breathe lying down, you can do it while seated on a chair and eventually do it whenever and wherever you want.

- ***Breath-focus technique:*** In this technique, there are focus words and phrases in use. The idea is to choose a focus word that makes you feel relaxed, smile or feel neutral, and focus on it repeatedly. Examples include such words as relax, peace and joy. Practice your breath focus for about 10 minutes a session, then work your way up. For this exercise, you can either sit or lie down in a place that is comfortable, then, without trying to change how you are breathing, bring awareness to your breath. Next, alternate between deep breaths and normal ones, paying attention to how your abdomen expands as you deeply inhale and practice deep breathing. Place a hand below your belly button, relax and notice the rise and fall with each inhalation and exhalation, respectively. Loudly sigh with each exhalation. Start breath-focusing by combining deep breathing with a focus word, phrase or imagery that will help you to relax. For example, you can assume that the air you inhale is calmness and peace, while the one you exhale is anxiety and tension.

- *Alternate nostril breathing:* Popularly known as nodi shodhana, it is best practiced before meals and is effective for enhancing cardiovascular function and lowering heart rate. If you are congested or sick, you may want to avoid this exercise, since you need to keep your breath smooth and even throughout. The exercise is simple. Find a comfortable position when seated and lift your right hand to the nose only pressing the first and middle fingers to the palm while the rest are extended. Gently close the right nostril after an exhale, inhaling through the left nostril before closing it with the right ring and pinky fingers. In essence, the thumb closes the right nostril while the ring and pinky fingers close the left nostril. Next, release the thumb and exhale through the right nostril before inhaling again through it, then closing it.

Open the left nostril and exhale. Keep the cycle going for up to five minutes. Remember to end the session with an exhalation on the left side.

- *Lion's breath:* No, you are not turning into a lion, but wouldn't you want to have its energy? The lion's breath not only energizes you but also relieves tension in your face and chest. Simply find a comfortable seated position either on your heels or cross-legged. Spread your fingers wide and press the palms against your knees then inhale deeply through the nose with eyes wide open. Open your mouth wide, stick out your tongue and bring its tip towards the chin. Next, contract your frontal throat muscles and exhale through the mouth producing a long "ha" sound. Then, turn your gaze to the space at your nose's tip or between your eyebrows. Repeat this two to three times and feel the energy flow within you.

- *Equal breathing:* If you are feeling particularly unbalanced, then this is the breathing exercise for you. The focus is on making your inhales and exhales the same length, steady and smooth to give you balance and equanimity. The breath length should also be neither too difficult nor easy, but also fast enough to maintain through the practice, usually for 3-5 counts. For this, find a comfortable seated position, then use your nose to breathe in and out. Count the time during each inhale, and ensure the exhale gets similar time. You can choose to have a slight pause after each inhale and exhale. Keep up the cycle for at least five minutes.

- *Coherent/resonant breathing:* Here, you take five full breaths each minute by inhaling and exhaling for a count of five. Resonant breathing not only maximizes your HRV (Heart Rate Variability), but it also reduces stress, as well as symptoms of depression. All you have to do is inhale for a count to five and exhale for a similar count, then keep going for a few minutes.

- *Deep breathing:* You may have heard the phrase, "Take a deep breath." Taking a deep breath helps to keep you centered and relaxed, and it sure works. You can do this while sitting or standing. Drawing your elbows back slightly allows your chest to expand. Inhale deeply through the nose and hold for a count of 55 before slowly releasing the breath through the nose. You can repeat this until you feel sufficiently relaxed and able to deal with whatever the situation.

- **Sitali breath:** This is also a good breathing exercise for relaxing your mind. Find a comfortable seated position, then stick your tongue out and curl it bringing in the outer edges together. If your tongue is stubborn and refuses to oblige, simply purse your lips. Inhale through the mouth, and exhale through the nose. Repeat the cycle for about five minutes.

- **Humming bee breath:** If you ever need instant calm, then this is the breathing exercise for you. It also helps to relieve anxiety, anger and frustration. The only flip side is that you do need to sound like a humming bee, so choose your place well for this exercise. After picking a comfortable seated position, relax your face and close your eyes, then put the first finger on the tragus cartilage, which partially covers the ear canal. Breathe in and, as you breathe out, gently press into the cartilage, then hum loudly. Keep going until you feel comfortable or calm enough.

2. Mindfulness Meditation

For those suffering from anxiety, pain and depression, you can get reprieve and be able to relax through mindfulness meditation. You only need to find a comfortable sitting position, then focus on your breathing. The key thing here is to bring your mind's attention to the present moment. It helps if you find a good relaxing place like a park, forest or the riverbank to do this. Focus on the current moment without allowing your mind to drift to the past and what you could have done or should have done. Also, this is not the time to start worrying about the future, its concerns and what it will bring. The time now is to focus on the present, taking in the environment and allowing yourself to relax. Many people have experienced the joy of mindful meditation, making it one of the most popular methods of relaxation. I am also a great supporter of this technique as it is one of the surest ways to breathe in, take in the moment and relax.

3. Tai Chi, Yoga and Qigong

Not only do these three ancient arts come loaded with physical and beauty benefits, but they also have the ability to focus your thoughts in a way that distracts racing thoughts and helps you to relax. Besides, they also enhance your balance and flexibility. If you generally do not lead an active life or have health problems, you may want to stay away from these. However, with a good trainer, you can begin from the beginner level and build up as you experience both mind relaxation and fitness. It is recommended that you check with your doctor before beginning these exercises.

4. Guided scenery

We all naturally want to associate with good things, soothing scenes and experiences. However, life throws many other difficult experiences and situations at us that can potentially push us into a world of negativity and self-doubt. At such times, you can pull out the gilded scenery technique. Here you conjure up images of soothing places, scenes and experiences that can help you to focus and relax. The good news is that there are different applications and recordings available online that have calming scenes for you to choose from. Ensure you choose what calms you down, has personal significance and makes you feel positive. Through guided imagery, you reinforce positivity within yourself, keeping away the negative thoughts and helping you to relax. You focus your attention on the image, or scene and relax into the moment clearing your mind of the negativity and going into a positive and soothing mood. The technique is particularly useful and calming to those with intrusive thoughts or who find it difficult to conjure up positive mental images.

5. Repetitive Prayer

If you are one of those people who are not very keen on religion, this may not be the best technique for you. However, you can attest that in times of need, darkness and hopelessness, we all tend to say a prayer. The idea behind this technique is to silently repeat a phrase or a short prayer while performing breath focus. If you are particularly religious or spiritual, you will draw more meaning from this technique as it appeals to your spirit, as well as the mind. You can even opt to add some of the religious items, like a rosary or praying beads, to make the experience wholesome. Adding breathing exercises ensures that the combination is relaxing. If you are not quite the spiritual or the religious type, you can repeat a positive phrase or a paragraph over and over until you feel relaxed and at peace. The constant repeating helps your mind to focus and absorb the positive message and leave aside the intrusive thoughts or anxiety.

6. Body Scan

There are no big machines to get into for the scan. Instead, this technique combines breath focus with focused muscle relaxation. You need to start with deep breathing, as we learned earlier on, until you feel sufficiently comfortable. The next step is to focus on either a group of muscles or one part of the body at any given time. You mentally release any tension that you may feel in these muscles or part of the body while still on breath focus. The reason it is called a body scan is because you move from one part to the next, releasing the tension until you feel relaxed everywhere. In the process, you will grow aware of the connection between body and mind and appreciate how interrelated they are. Pay special attention to the areas that you feel are strained, like your eyes or head. As soon as you are done, you will be amazed at how light you feel and how much mental weight you will have shed, leaving you relaxed.

7. Exercise

Most people who work out regularly know the benefits of exercise. However, if you are not one of them, you may consider it to be more trouble. Exercise is one of the most effective ways of combating stress, anxiety, depression and intrusive thoughts, while gaining the benefits of having a healthier, fit and more beautiful body. As weird as it sounds, putting yourself through physical stress relieves mental stress and helps you to relax and feel good.

By exercising you lower your body's stress hormones, like cortisol, while promoting the release of endorphins, which make you feel good, are natural painkillers and improve your mood. Additionally, exercise improves your sleep quality, something that those battling with mental illness would really appreciate. Sleep can be elusive, and even when present, it involves much tossing and turning. Exercise can sort the sleep issue making you relaxed and energetic when you get up. Moreover, exercise comes with a body to die for, one that you are proud of and thus boosts your confidence, contributing to your mental well-being.

With exercise, you do not have to become a top athlete, although that is also welcome. You need to choose an exercise routine that works for you, something that you enjoy, and you can do often. For example, you can begin taking walks that help to soothe you and appreciate the environment. You can also opt for swimming, yoga, hiking or even dancing. Find whatever exercise makes you happy. You do not have to know how to do it; enjoy the learning process and notice how relaxed you get, losing both physical and mental baggage.

8. Light a candle

You do not have to be a hopeless romantic to light a candle. Get a candle with a soothing scent, like lavender, rose, sandalwood, neroli, vetiver, Roman chamomile, Geranium, Ylang ylang, Bergamot, Orange or

Frankincense. The art of using these scents in improving your mood is referred to as aromatherapy, which has been known to improve sleep, reduce anxiety and make you relaxed. The calming scents will help you relax and lift off any negative emotions. You can light a candle while taking a shower, or even during a delicious meal or in your living room or bedroom.

9. Write it down

We have already talked in depth about the topic of journaling. Writing down your thoughts and emotions is one of the most effective ways of relaxing, as it lifts the mental stress and gives you an opportunity to replace the negative thoughts with positive ones.

10. Join great company

Often people get stressed, anxious, sink further into depression and host all their intrusive thoughts because of being alone and brooding. You can easily escape all these and enjoy fun times with family and friends. You have to carefully choose those that come with a good vibe and bring out the best in you. Having good social support is a great way to pull through mental illness and stressful situations. Women particularly benefit from social support, as they release oxytocin, which is a natural stress reliever.

Alternatively, you can choose to spend time with a support group for people battling mental illness. Ensure that you are with people that understand your condition and urge you to get out of it or those who have done so successfully. The idea is to keep your outlook positive.

11. Say No

Sit and think back to the hardest times you have had, and you will realize that they most likely emanated from your inability to say no. You may find that you pile your plate too high with other people's problems, concerns and activities that you can say no to. You could be financially constrained because you gave your money to someone else. Your work life may be stressful because you are intent on helping others.

Only take on what is comfortable for you to do, and say no to everything that will put unnecessary stress on you. You will find that your life is more relaxed, and you are more productive and less stressed.

12. Laugh

When you are laughing, your worries, anxieties, stresses and stressors disappear. There is relaxing power in laughing, in addition to relieving stress and tension. Laughing also puts you in a good mood, enabling you to relax.

Call that one friend who cracks you up or hang out with some good friends and family. If you are not in the mood for dealing with people, watch a funny show on TV or even those hilarious clips on YouTube. You should be happy and relaxed in no time.

Chapter Summary

In this chapter, we have looked at various ways you can relax even when you feel like the weight of the world is on your shoulder. We learned that:

- Breathing exercises are some of the most effective ways of relaxing. There are many different modes of breathing for relaxation, including the lion's breath and deep breathing.
- You can also engage in mindful meditation, yoga or even guided scenery, among others.
- You do not have to use one of these techniques. You can try different combinations until you find what works best for you.

In the next chapter, you will learn another CBT technique that can help you in fighting anxiety, depression and intrusive thoughts. It is simply by having fun!

Chapter Eight

Technique 6 – Have Fun

Have you ever realized how our activities influence our mood? For instance, if you listen to sad songs, you get sad and fall into a low mood. On the other hand, if you listen to lively music, you will end up dancing to it and generally feeling happy, alive and energetic. If you spend most of your time among negative people or depressing situations, you are likely to end up feeling stressed or depressed. Looking at the trend, therefore, it is important to fill your days with positivity and to schedule activities that you enjoy. In a world filled with stress, you have to create a small piece of heaven for yourself. One way of learning to do so is through a CBT technique called activity scheduling and behavioral activation.

What is activity scheduling and behavioral activation?

Most of the activities that we have to do for our survival are mainly challenging and not very pleasant. You may need to find a way to create some positivity and fun in your life by scheduling as well as participating in positive events that boost your mood. Activity scheduling and behavioral activation is an evidence-based CBT technique that is effective in the reduction of a number of mental-health symptoms.

When you are suffering from a mental-health condition, you may want to stay away from people, preferring to wallow in your pain and not deal with any social issues. You will tend to isolate yourself and cancel engaging activities, even those that you previously enjoyed, as well as decline invitations by colleagues, friends and family. While you may think of this as a way of reducing pressure on yourself, it increases your depression making it intense and last longer and subsequently making you want to isolate yourself even more.

A good way of breaking the cycle is identifying an activity that boosts your mood, like swimming, having dinner with a friend, watching a live match or even going to the gym. Your therapist can work with you in picking a positive and engaging activity to do. The therapist, however, does not help in picking any random and fun activity. He helps in the identification of the value of these activities and rank them. For instance, he may check how work, volunteering, family, friendship, intimacy, entertainment or health, among others, are of value to you. He will then help you to gather activities that support what you value the most. For example, if you value friendships, you may be interested in having coffee with a friend. On the other hand, if you value health and fitness, going to the gym may be most appealing to you.

Once you engage in the activity, you can review how it affected your mood. If you find that you are feeling much better than before, then you can continue scheduling the activity or find a similar one to keep your mood light.

How does it work?

Scheduling an activity that is pleasant and fun can help you be better by providing you with something to look forward to. The boost in mood starts immediately from the planning stage and all the way to the time for the activity.

Engaging in a pleasant activity that adds value to your life will certainly cause you to experience a bright mood. You will feel great at having done something beneficial yet fun which can help you break out of the terrible mood you have sustained for so long. You may find that you are now willing to engage in other similar activities.

How to effectively enhance activity scheduling and behavioral activation

Activity scheduling and behavioral activation may sound like a simple coping skill, but you may find yourself struggling to get it done particularly when unmotivated. After some time in isolation, you get used to your own presence, and breaking away from this cycle can be pretty difficult. Below are some of the ways that can get you started on scheduling pleasant activities.

- *Go for activities that are personally important:* Sometimes, we are tempted to live for other people. You may choose to have a coffee date with a friend because that friend has been pushing for it or choose an activity that will make your partner happy. Remember, the focal person here is you so choose activities that are of importance to you to get your motivation up. Ensure that you go for activities that you are connected to and engaged with and that bring you joy. The objective is for you to have fun, feel good and fulfill some of your desires.

- ***Choose specific activities with measurable progress:*** Do not opt for blanket activities but rather choose something with which you can easily track the progress. You have to be able to know that you completed a task and review it. For example, instead of planning to get fit, be specific. Plan to either go to the gym for an hour or jump rope for 10 minutes. You can hold yourself accountable and be proud of what you achieve, which will further motivate you to go further. Achieving your goals will also lift your mood.

- ***Start from the easiest to the most difficult activities:*** When you are anxious about something or generally feeling low, you may find behavioral activation as being quite hard. A way to ease you into it is to just get started. If you are to go out for coffee, you can begin by simply taking a shower, then pat yourself on the back for that. If you don't get moving, you can easily find that avoidance behaviors begin to set in. List all your activities from the easiest and begin with that. As you keep going, you will realize it is not as hard as you thought it would be. Soon, you will get immersed in the activity and go on to complete it. Additionally, starting with the easy tasks ensures that you do not get overwhelmed.

- *Ask for support:* Occasionally, it is hard to pull yourself out of the rut that comes with mental illness. You may want to attend to those fun activities, but you lack the strength and will to do so. At such times, do not be afraid to ask for help from people in your support circle. Tell a trusted friend or family member what you plan to achieve during the week and ask them to be your accountability partner. They can check in on how far you have gone, encourage you and be your cheerleader. In the end, you get to have fun, even if there are small steps at the start.

- *Spice it up:* They say that variety is the spice of life, so don't be boring. The whole objective is to get you out of that gloomy room and get some adrenaline and feel-good hormones flowing through you. Mix up different types of activities across varying life sectors, like fitness, entertainment and work. The more activities you plan, the more likely you are to have more fun and get into a better mood. Besides, doing one thing repetitively will wear you down and slump you back to the world of gloom.

- **Be mindful:** Have you driven home, yet your mind is elsewhere and full of other things? Similarly, you can be engaging in a fun activity, yet you are not having any fun. Your mind is engaged elsewhere worrying about your future or ruminating about the past. Being present and mindful is crucial in having real fun and enjoying the various benefits of engaging in behavioral activation. Choose suitable activities, be present and have lots of fun.

- **Go slow at first:** You can hardly manage to fit in so many activities after you are used to sleeping most of the time. Be kind to yourself and take things slowly, enjoying one activity at a time before adding another. You need to realize that the anxiety and depression will not wear off immediately. Take things slowly, and build your motivation, then move ahead.

- **Take note of and reward progress:** The day you finally step into the gym after a long time, note it down somewhere and give yourself a reward for taking that first and bold step. Every time you make any progress, reward yourself as a form of motivation to keep going.

Chapter Summary

In this chapter, we have looked at how important having fun is in improving mental health. We learned that:

- You should start by scheduling activities that are fun for you and those that have added value.
- If you need any form of motivation to either get started or keep going, do not be afraid to ask for help from your support circle.
- Do not strain yourself. The objective is to have fun.

In the next chapter, you will learn another CBT technique that can help you in fighting anxiety, depression and intrusive thoughts brought about by the beliefs we so dearly hold. It is time to test the beliefs!

Chapter Nine

Technique 7 – Testing the Beliefs

When we hold onto a belief for so long, we tend to think it's true, actually we just know it is a valid belief. These beliefs can occupy a huge part of our lives and shape the way we live our lives and relate to others. While having beliefs is a good thing and can help anchor us within life, they should not affect our daily lives, work and trouble us socially. If you are not living your best life because of beliefs, then it may be time to check if they are true and if they are worth the disruption to your life.

One of the most powerful tools available in CBT is behavioral experiments. The experiments are simply planned activities that aim to test the validity of those beliefs that you have. During this exercise, information is collected then used in testing your beliefs about yourself, others and the world. The method can also be used to test new and adaptive beliefs. You can think of behavioral experiments much like the scientific studies that prove a certain element is either as you make it to be or not.

The value of testing beliefs is that you are involved in the process and thus are not simply being told of the results. You gather the information and test the belief so its validity is clear to you without a doubt. You are, therefore, able to shed off some of the useless and inhibiting beliefs and replace those with positive beliefs.

Types of Behavioral Experiments

There are different ways you can test those beliefs that you hold based on the purpose. Some of these include:

1. ***Surveys:*** They can provide you with information on the belief you are testing. The method is helpful when you have a belief about what others think. For example, one belief could be that you believe that people will not like you if they know you suffer from anxiety.

2. ***Experiential exercises:*** They allow you to put specific beliefs to the test. For example, "If I

exercise, I will pass out." You can engage in some exercise to see if it is true.

3. ***Hypothesis testing:*** This can be designed in a way that allows you to not only collect information but also use it in the testing of the validity of your beliefs, predictions and thoughts. Hypothesis testing may involve:

- *Hypothesis A Testing:* Tests an existing and potentially unhelpful belief. For example, you may think that by exercising, you will pass out.

- *Hypothesis B Testing:* Tests a new belief. For instance, you may decide to embrace saying no. Try saying no when you're uncomfortable with something, then observe the results.

- *Hypothesis A vs. Hypothesis B:* This is a test between the original and the newly constructed belief to find out which one is better. For example, A could be, "Saying yes earns me more friends and respect," vs. B, "Saying no when I'm uncomfortable and being assertive earns me respect." You therefore test the two to see which one gives you the desired results, then adopt it.

4. ***Direct observation:*** Sometimes you may have a belief that you are not comfortable testing yourself. For example, you may believe that people do not care about others and, if anything were to happen to you in the streets, people would pass right by you without offering help. If the fear is deeply set, you may find it difficult to test it. You can have someone else test it for you and you observe. For instance, your friend can pretend to collapse on the street as you observe how many people, if any, come to his aid.

5. ***Gathering information:*** There are many sources of information in today's world. The Internet, for instance, is full of information that you can use to prove or disprove your belief. For example, if you believe that the snowcaps will all melt and wash out the land all around causing massive deaths, it could help to research more on snowcaps and even watch how intense the melting process is and how many people are affected each year by the same. Information is power.

6. ***Discovery experiments:*** There are times when you can hold a feared belief so much that you just know if you do that, things will not be OK, but you cannot even explain how they will be.

For example, you may believe that if you step out of the house after seven in the evening, something bad will happen, but you do not know what or why. You are not certain about what to test here. With support, you can step out and take an evening walk to see what happens.

How to carry out a behavioral experiment

a) *Identification of target cognition*

You need to identify the target cognition as precisely as possible, including assessing how strongly you believe in this. You can use the 'If...then' formula. "If I exercise, then I will pass out."

Also, identify the safety behaviors you have put in place. For example, one such behavior could be that you always wear a reflector jacket when crossing the road. While you are here, also think through what you think would happen if you did not wear that reflector jacket.

Rate how deep your conviction is on a scale of 0-10, with 10 being that you're absolutely sure.

Now that you know what you are dealing with, we can move to the next step.

b) Design the Experiment

Depending on the belief, determine what will be the best way to test it, bearing in mind your readiness, safety and any other practicalities. You may also need to think of the occurrence of any other problems during the experiment. You should also check whether you are prepared to forego some of the safety behaviors for the success of the experiment.

Designing an experiment may take much mental effort, especially on the need to step out of your comfort zone. You may want to have another person help you in this phase. A therapist is a good choice.

Go ahead and undertake the experiment with an open mind.

c) Outcome and Learning

After the experiment, you need to take time to make meaning of what happened, as well as the data that you may have collected. Ask yourself, "What happened?" "What have you learned?" "Is there any change to your belief?" "Have you learned anything about yourself?" "Is there a better way of looking at things?" "Does the outcome support your original belief?" "Are there any contradictions?" "What are the implications of the test?" "Does it affect your daily life?"

d) *Way forward*

Take time to reflect on the outcome as well as what you have learned, then design a way forward. Some of the questions you can ask yourself include: "What have you learned from the experiment that can be replicated in other situations?" "What other experiments can you do?" "What do you need to do to maintain what you have learned?" "Have you developed a new perspective, and can it be tested?" "How do you put what you learned into practice?" "What else should you test?"

The purpose of testing these beliefs is to break any negative ones that you may be holding on to and, hence, free you from them. You can then enjoy life without unnecessary worries.

Chapter Summary

In this chapter, we have looked at how you can improve your mental health by testing those beliefs that seem to be disruptive to your life. We have learned that:

There are different methods that you can use to test your beliefs, such as discovery experiments, surveys, hypothesis testing and direct observation.

- Similar to a true scientist, you need to be acutely aware of what belief you are testing.
- You also need to ensure that you think through the testing process, including what could go wrong and the necessary safety measures.
- After results, it is important to review and reflect, including the lessons learned.
- You also have to incorporate the lessons into your life, otherwise what was the purpose of testing the belief in the first place?

In the next chapter, you will learn another CBT technique that can help you in fighting anxiety and intrusive thoughts through role-play.

Chapter Ten

Technique 8 – Role-Playing

Another technique that is useful in alleviating mental illnesses and offering you a happier easier life is role-playing. Sometimes you may become so anxious about an event that you find yourself panicking and unable to focus. You may be so anxious and stressed that you dread waking up in the morning. Other times, you may have a fear of something that is so bad that it affects your everyday life. At such time, you can benefit from a CBT technique called role-playing.

Role-playing helps you to develop a deep understanding or change within yourself. With this technique, you get an opportunity to perform certain behavior or act in a controlled, safe and risk-free environment. When role-playing, you can reenact yourself, another person, situation or circumstance, including your reactions. You can then get feedback either from a group, if you are working with a group, or a therapist or another individual.

Role-play mainly occurs in the present. You have to put yourself in the situation and reenact it as if it is happening now. Here, you do not work with either the future or the present, but just the present. Role-playing may be challenging as you start, as it requires you to fit into a certain role. You can start by reenacting the scenes that are easy, then move on to more complex ones.

How to Implement Role-Playing

Elements of Role Playing

As a prerequisite to role-playing, you need to understand the four main elements.

1. *The Encounter:* You need to be able to understand other people's perspective, as you may be required to play them in a certain situation.
2. *The Stage:* Refers to the space usually filled with simple props that provide a realistic experience.
3. *The Soliloquy:* As the name suggests, it is a speech in which you express your private

thoughts, as well as the associated feelings. You are likely to come across your irrational beliefs here.

4. *Doubling:* Can really help you to have increased awareness, and it occurs when another person stands behind you when you are reenacting a scene and helps to express any thoughts and feelings that you do not express.

Phases of Role Playing

Knowing these elements sets you up for role-playing. There is, however, more that you should learn. There are phases that you should go through when role-playing. These are:

- *Situation identification:* You have to correctly identify the situation to be reenacted as clearly as possible so that you know what you are dealing with and the potential outcomes.

- *The details:* The more detailed the situation is, the better the role-play can be and the better the results. Include all the necessary details. If it is in a coffee shop, consider even other patrons and what to order. Having tea or wine may contribute differently to the situation.

- *Warm-up phase:* Much like traditional acting, you need to connect with the situation and think through the emotions you will need in order to be able to reenact. You may choose to warm up either physically by doing a run-through of the situation or by doing so mentally. Ensure you are in the right frame of mind before beginning role-playing.

- *Action phase:* Here, you go over the details of the situation with the rest of the group, if in a group session or with the therapist, or even a friend. You also set the scene, paying attention to making it as realistic as possible and not using your imagination. You then reenact the situation, practically moving from your role to that of any other person in the situation. You have to ensure you are as practical and as realistic as possible. Having someone else there helps to ensure that you do not project your imagined worries or emotions.

- *Sharing and analysis:* The next phase involves sharing the lessons learned during the role-play. You can think of it as a reflective phase that looks back at the role-play and processes what happened.

- *Reenactment:* You can now repeat the exercise, paying attention to targeted behavior until you feel confident. For example, if you are role-playing a social situation and learning how to behave in such a manner that you are not overly anxious or a misfit, you can continually practice until you are confident and can socially fit in without many challenges.

- *Follow-up:* You need to regularly keep tabs on your progress. If you are handling the social scene much better, note that so you can celebrate the wins while working on the weaknesses.

Variations in Role Playing

There are different variations of role-play that you can use. Some of them include:

- *Behavioral rehearsal:* This involves rewarding and reinforcing the target behavior when you perform it. If you perform as expected without having negative behavior, you get a reward from a friend or even your therapist. You can even award yourself. The behavior is then reinforced through this method.

- *The mirror technique:* Works well in group-therapy sessions. Here, if you are reenacting a scene and critical behavior occurs, you have to take a seat. Someone else now comes in to take your place and reenacts the scene, usually exaggeratedly. You watch and can then evaluate his response, noting his mistakes. You can then agree on a better way of responding for you to practice.

- *The Gestalt variation:* The method is mainly used by Gestalt therapists and makes use of two chairs standing in for other people. The chairs stand for you and anyone else you have an issue with, therefore their logic and desire. Your work is to sit in one chair and speak from the chair's (person's) point of view, expressing his thoughts and feelings.

- *Costume role-playing:* Works well with children and simply involves wearing different costumes during different roles. You, therefore, are keenly aware of who you are during the role-playing.

Benefits of Role Playing

We role-play often in our lives even when we do not have any phobias or anxiety issues to deal with.

When you have a big interview, you may find yourself reenacting the scene in your head and practicing your responses. You may also stand in front of the mirror and practice asking that girl out on a date or how to react when you meet an important person. From these examples, you can tell that you are likely to be role-playing when nervous or anxious about something.

Role-playing is helpful in making you more confident when facing a certain situation, which in turn reduces the associated stress and anxiety. Since you have prepared for all scenarios, you feel able to deal with the situation.

Additionally, role-playing helps you to tackle both difficult and unfamiliar topics, as well as have emotionally difficult conversations, especially in conflict resolution. By reenacting the situation, you get a chance to address the issues before facing the actual situations. You are therefore better prepared for whichever direction the situation may take and the different ways they may respond. Since they do not catch you off guard, you can handle the situation well. Moreover, by going through the situation beforehand, you become aware of which responses can be counter-productive so you can avoid them.

Another benefit of role-playing is that it helps you get in touch with your feelings and thoughts about a situation in a way that helps you to clearly assess it without hiding your true feelings. You also get a clear view of how others feel about the situation and, hence, know how to approach things.

Role-playing also builds empathy and helps to improve communication skills, as well as sensitivity to the feelings and thoughts of others. Since you are not in denial, and you have insights into how the other person feels and what their perspective is, you are in a better position to communicate effectively and resolve any existing conflicts.

Aside from phobias, role-playing is an important technique in treating anxiety by preparing you for the world outside. The good news is that, if you are honest with yourself, you can role-play any situation and be better placed to handle whatever life throws at you.

Don't shy away

An interesting fact about role-playing is that it can feel stupid. Yes, you feel stupid standing in front of the mirror in your bedroom. Now, imagine having to reenact a scene among other people? The start is not easy, and you may need encouragement to continue, but you will be glad you did.

I role-play a lot. Every time I have a big event or a potentially difficult situation that I have to face, I role-play. From the exercise, I emerge strong and confident knowing that I have covered many of the bases, and I am ready for however the situation plays out.

Role-playing also calls for you to be very honest. Speaking or acknowledging our inner thoughts is no small feat, but it is something you have to do. You have to look within and not edit the thoughts and feelings. You also have to wear the other party's shoes and walk in them, acknowledging where the shoe pinches even when you know you have caused the pinch. In these times, it is recommended that you have a support system or join a group therapy where you can have someone point out those emotions that you may not feel confident enough to bring out. My time in therapy has taught me that honesty, particularly being honest with yourself, is a key component of the healing process.

Take time to role-play, whether alone or with others. You will realize that you grow mentally and emotionally stronger, empathize more, communicate better and become more confident.

Chapter Summary

In this chapter, we have looked at role-playing and its role in reducing anxiety, symptoms of depression and equipping you with confidence to go through life. We have learned that:

- Role-playing involves reenacting a scene or a situation, so you can look deeply into your feelings and thoughts.
- Role-playing always happens at the present.
- Through this technique, you are able to put yourself in another person's shoes and thus better understand him/her.
- It equips you with confidence to handle situations since you know what to expect.

In the next chapter, you will learn another CBT technique that can help you stop being overwhelmed by tasks by simply breaking them down.

Chapter Eleven

Technique 9 – Simply Break It Down

Have you ever dreaded the day ahead even before you embark on it? It could be that you have tasks that feel overwhelming, which stresses you out, makes you feel small, incompetent and unworthy? The truth is that we all feel overwhelmed at some point, but when it wears you down so much you begin to feel dysfunctional, then it is time to address this concern.

Some people have a difficult time completing a task. They may lack the necessary skills or are not familiar with it. Occasionally, the task may feel overwhelming and hard to do, resulting in stress, anxiety and a foul mood. If you are finding it difficult to complete tasks or reach your goals, do not despair; there is hope and treatment for you through successive approximation.

In simple terms, successive approximation is a CBT technique that calls for you to break down your tasks so they become easier to manage, and you can then work toward completing your goals. Instead of taking up the entire project or task, split it into smaller and easily manageable tasks that build up to get the whole project done. If you have anxieties that make it difficult for you to undertake any of the tasks that you need to, you can employ successive approximations.

Parts of Successive Approximations

In most parts, successive approximation is a simple yet effective technique that you can use at home to get things going while reducing the associated stress and anxiety. However, there are steps that you can follow to ease the process. After the initial step, you can do the other steps not in any particular order.

- ***Identify the task at hand:*** You have to be clear on what you want to do and achieve. Ensure that you know exactly what the task entails, including the details, so you do not leave anything undone. You do not want to complete the task only to find that there are some aspects not done.

- **Setting subgoals:** You want to modify your non-functional behavior into the desired behavior by successive approximations. Here, you break down the main task into smaller tasks that you can tick off as you go. Think of it as a staircase and you have to go up one step at a time to the next. For example, you may want to paint your exterior window frames, but are afraid of climbing up the ladder. The fear may be valid after falling down and breaking a leg four years ago. Since then, you have not been up a ladder, yet now you need to use one. Set your subgoals to be something like climbing up a step higher each day.

- **Put the tasks in a chronological order:** After you have split up the tasks into smaller ones, it is important that you arrange them in chronological order, so you are aware of what you need to do next and don't skip any important subtasks. For example, if you are going out for a work party and dread the social interaction, you can arrange to pack your bag, choose an outfit, iron your clothes, take a shower, put on your clothes, call a cab and grab your bag, among the other items you need to go out. Since you are nervous, chances of forgetting something are high. You do not want to arrive at the party after all the effort only to realize that you did not comb your hair. You will instantly feel like a loser, the same thoughts that we are working at avoiding.

- ***Identify triggers:*** With a good plan in place, you do not want the kind of surprises that neutralize all the hard work. You need to identify those triggers that will make you bail out on the task or those that demoralize you so they can be managed. For example, if seeing bandages will cause you to not attempt climbing the ladder, avoid them at all costs. If the triggers are in your head or among your friends, you want to stay away from that friend for that period.

- ***Identify the sensitive aspects:*** In most of these situations, you will realize that there are some sensitive aspects of which you should be aware. For example, you may find that some of the sensitive aspects when going for a party include your getting dressed, your ability to socialize and the menu. Knowing this will ensure that you are well-prepared to deal with them. You can opt to ask for professional help when choosing your outfit and settle for one that does not attract much attention. You can also role-play as you prepare for the party and ask about the menu in advance to make mental choices of what to have.

- *Commit:* You can't make much progress without making any commitment to the process. You have to ensure that you are willing to go through the subtasks to ensure that the entire process is done, then you can claim victory.

Steps for Successive Approximation Technique

1. *Find the starting place:* When facing a task—no matter how overwhelming—you will realize that it is not all bleak. There are parts of it that you can do without raising your anxiety level. For you to find the starting point for successive approximation, you have to find where your anxiety levels begin to go up. For example, if you are to climb the ladder and find out that even the sight of the ladder gets you very anxious, then that becomes your starting point. However, if you can climb the first two steps without feeling anxious, then the third step becomes your starting point.

2. *Withdraw when anxiety begins:* Once you know where to start, gather your courage and begin the journey. However, once your anxiety begins, withdraw immediately and head back to

the comfort zone. If the first two steps on the ladder are comfortable for you to take, but you experience mild anxiety as soon as one foot finds the next step, you need to step back to where you feel safe. Take some time to take a breath and relax. This would be a good time to practice some of those breathing exercises before trying again when you feel ready to do so.

3. *Overcoming:* As you continue to practice and keep doing the subtasks one a time, you will feel better as you see progress. You will also gain more confidence to keep going through the list of tasks and ultimately achieve your purpose. Once you have achieved the first task, you will realize that you can keep repeating and even enjoying doing it. Take time to appreciate the progress and reward yourself for learning a new behavior.

The beauty of breaking down the tasks is that it simplifies each task and reduces any undue pressure that you may be under. You are likely to do much more than you have done in years when you apply successive approximation.

As you engage in this exercise, it is important that you are kind to yourself, allowing time for you to gain courage to keep going. Don't expect that it will instantaneously work, enabling you to do so much, you may need to take the time to go through the subtasks. Therefore, while you may have a target to achieve, save yourself the extra pressure that comes with strict deadlines. If you are able to accomplish a subtask, pat yourself on the back.

Chapter Summary

In this chapter, we have looked at how simpler life and tasks can be if we break them down. Similar to how we cut our food into bite-sized chunks, it is important to also break down our tasks, especially those that seem overwhelming and difficult, into subtasks, then implement them one by one. We have also learned that:

- We should only undertake a task when we feel ready to do it. Piling on additional pressure will be counterproductive.
- Arrange the subtasks in chronological order where possible to avoid missing a task, which will be demoralizing.
- If you need help, ask for support. Some tasks take a lot of guts, especially in the face of past failure or hurt. Ask for support when you need it.
- Once you accomplish a task, take time to reward yourself, then keep practicing.

In the next chapter, you will learn another CBT technique, which can help to keep you in the present and prevent your thoughts from wandering into volatile zones, called mindfulness.

Chapter Twelve

Technique 10 – Mindfulness

Our minds ideally should concentrate on the task at hand except that they occasionally veer off and bring in everyone and everything they meet on the way. Have you ever been working on a project then your mind goes fishing for what would possibly go wrong or what someone thinks of you or the failures that came with the last project? You find yourself having moved from the task at hand to concentrating on those things that the mind brought in, yet you know they will cause you stress, anxiety and self-doubt. You can benefit from a CBT technique, called Mindfulness-Based Cognitive Therapy (MBCT).

What is MBCT?

MBCT is a technique that works by combining mindfulness strategies with cognitive behavioral techniques in helping you understand and manage your emotions and thoughts better and get reprieve from any distressing feelings. The technique works well for a variety of mental illnesses.

During psychotherapy, you combine cognitive therapy, mindfulness and meditation. Mindfulness refers to a state of focusing on being acutely aware of what you are feeling and sensing presently without judgment or interruption. Throughout the process, you will learn to recognize and understand your feelings and thought patterns, then you can create new and more effective ones.

In most cases, MBCT works as a group intervention lasting up to eight weeks, and, I must say, the time is worth it. You are required to have a two-hour weekly course and a day-long class sometime after the fifth week. While some of the learning happens in the session, most of the practice happens outside the sessions. You will have to do some homework that may include listening to guided meditations and cultivating mindfulness in your activities by applying the MBCT skills. You also get to learn the three-minute breathing space.

Three-Minute Breathing Space

Usually, this is a quick exercise that is done in three steps:

1. In the first minute, you ask yourself, "How am I doing right now?" while observing your experience and trying to find the right words for those thoughts, sensations and feelings.
2. During the second minute you focus on breath.
3. You spend the last minute expanding your attention from just your breath to the physical sensations and their effect on your body.

How does it work?

Through MBCT, you can tackle those intrusive thoughts by learning to use mindfulness mediation in disrupting the processes that often trigger those thoughts and emotions. Allowing such thoughts to happen leads to low mood, weariness, sluggishness, and negative thoughts taking over and that makes you anxious and depressed. Worse is that even after such an episode, there are chances that you may feel blue, and small other things, like fatigue, can easily trigger another episode.

In this technique, you learn to recognize that you are a separate entity from your mood and thought, giving you a sense of being. Understanding that your thoughts and emotions do not define you can help you allow you to be liberated from negative thought patterns that may be playing on repeat mode in your head. You begin to appreciate your thoughts and emotions but also know that they are separate from you and although they can both exist simultaneously, they do not have to lead you where they please. You can go in the opposite direction—into the land of positivity—which disarms the negative ones. You are the one who matters, the one who decides what to give power to.

You also learn various skills in MBCT that help you in combating those low, blue and depressive thoughts and symptoms as they arise. Learning MBCT skills helps you to have your own army and strategies that you can refer to when you feel like the mental battlefield is getting hot or overwhelming. Besides, knowing that you are prepared for such times of intrusive thoughts, anxiety and depression gives you confidence in your ability to deal with them, making you approach things from a winner's perspective.

Benefits of MBCT

There are many benefits of MBCT. Some of them include:

- Helps you discover your own mood and thought patterns.
- Helps you learn how to focus on the present and enjoy the small pleasures of life.
- Teaches you how to stop the downward spiral that comes with painful memories and bad moods.
- Learning how to shift to a balanced and non-judgmental mental state.
- Improved physical health, since most of the techniques include some form of exercise.
- Reduced stress that comes with focusing on the present and soothing exercises, like yoga.
- Improved concentration on tasks, increasing your chances of succeeding.
- Improved overall mood.
- Better ability to face the challenges of life.

MBCT Techniques

Other MBCT techniques include:

1. Body scan

Earlier on, we touched on the body scan. Here, you lie on your back with palms up and feet slightly apart or you sit comfortably on a chair with your feet on the floor. You have to stay very still during this exercise and only move deliberately, fully aware if you need to adjust your position.

Next, with the help of the facilitator, you bring awareness to your breath, taking note of the rhythm of inhaling and exhaling. Now, move attention to your body, take in everything about it, including how it feels, the clothing texture, temperature, contours of the surface you are lying on, and the entire environment. Once you have mastered that, focus your attention on any part of the body that is feeling light, heavy, sore or even tingly. Move any parts where you feel no sensation.

Scan the entire body, starting from the toes, paying attention to how each body part feels. Move up to the rest of the foot, up the legs and all the way to the top of the head. Once you finish scanning every bit of your body, gently bring back awareness to the room where you are, opening your eyes slowly and moving to a comfortable sitting position.

2. Mindful Stretching

You have to bring in mindfulness to your situations, and one way of doing so is incorporating it into your stretching. Before you rush to exercise, take time to have some mindful stretching, which prepares both your body and mind for the upcoming physical exertion. Besides, mindful stretching can help increase your sense of balance and awareness. Below are some mindful-stretching options you can try.

- ☐ *Pandiculation:* Means a fairly simple stretch. All you have to do is place your palms on your shoulders, raise your elbows to the height of the shoulders, then open your mouth to let out a satisfying yawn.

- ☐ *Yoga poses:* The four main ones are:

  1. *Side-to-side neck stretch:* Sit and gently use your hand to pull the neck from side to side.

  2. *Gomukhasana:* Open your chest as you extend the triceps and shoulders while sitting cross-legged or kneeling.

3. *Pigeon pose:* Your hips should be on the floor with one leg in front of you and perpendicular to the mat. The other leg stays straight out behind you.

4. *The scorpion:* Start by lying flat with your arms stretched out to the side. Lift your right foot high, keeping your sole straight up to the ceiling before lifting the right hip too. Now, move the lifted foot to the outside of the other leg, while keeping your arms and chest on the floor. You can then switch legs.

3. Mindful Showering

When you are just beginning, this is a good place to start, incorporating mindfulness in your daily activities. Give attention to the water temperature as it touches your body, feeling the spray, smell of the soap and the sensation of the lathered soap. If your mind begins to wander, as is common, steer it back to the present by focusing on what you are hearing, feeling, seeing and smelling.

4. Mindful Eating

Similarly, this involves giving all your attention to what you are eating. It helps if you can turn off things, like the TV, phone or radio, that are disruptive, so you can focus just on eating. Feel the texture of the food, concentrate on the aroma and the taste.

5. Mindfully Brushing Teeth

Don't laugh. Keeping in the present is important, and what better way to do so than focusing on the everyday activities that you undertake, especially brushing your teeth? Focus your attention on the strokes of the brush, their movement and feel on your teeth and gums. Give attention to the taste of the toothpaste and how it feels in your mouth.

In essence, you can incorporate mindfulness into all areas of life and your daily activities. By doing so, you learn to focus on the present, filter your thoughts to what you want then to be and, hence, exercise control over your thoughts and emotions. The main idea with mindfulness is not to change what you are doing but rather to pay attention and notice what you are doing. Gone will be the days you drove home and can't remember taking the last three turns or eating and not remembering the food's taste.

Learning to incorporate mindfulness in my life has been helpful in keeping me in the present, helping me appreciate the coffee, the sunshine, the flowers and all the simple beautiful things that life has to offer. I practice mindfulness so much in my daily life that it has become a part of me. When I feel those intrusive thoughts and anxiety about issues creeping in, I switch them off through mindfulness. I no longer go for coffee with a friend and spend the time worrying about work or things I haven't done. No, I sit there in the present, engage in the conversation, savor the coffee and the activities around the coffee shop. After that, I am glad I went out. I get to laugh, enjoy some good company and generally feel good. You should try it.

Chapter Summary

In this chapter, we have looked at how you can use mindfulness to gain control of your emotions and feelings, as well as stay in the present moment. We have seen how helpful this technique can be in alleviating symptoms of depression, reducing stress and anxiety, pushing away intrusive thoughts. We have also learned that:

- You can incorporate mindfulness in your day-to-day activities, like eating, breathing and walking.
- You can also practice mindful stretching, body scan and yoga, among others, to help you to re-focus and shed the negative thoughts and emotions.
- MBCT helps you to be able to face the challenges of life by providing you with useful techniques that you can follow to fight off negative emotions and incorporate positive ones.

Chapter Thirteen

Technique 11 – Play the Entire Script

———— ♦ ◇ ♦ ————

You probably know those thoughts that refuse to leave, at least not without a fight. The kind that sticks around long enough to convince you that they are legit, and you should be prepared for the worst. The kind that slowly creep in your head and, before long, they are deteriorating. For example, you ask a colleague to have coffee with you, and he agrees. Then the thought strikes, "He won't show up. He doesn't even like working with me. Leaves me alone to have coffee." Before long, the thought has graduated to, "Nobody even likes working with me. I am a horrible person. Nobody loves me." Soon, you find yourself in a foul mood, feeling stressed, anxious and with many other intrusive thoughts flying in and out as they please.

When you are catastrophizing, you see only the possibility of a disaster happening, even when there are no indications, or you take any small sign to indicate that bad things will happen. You also tend to jump to conclusions without evidence. If you are one of these people that suffer from anxiety and fear and only imagine the worst-case scenario, then you need a CBT technique that simply tells you to play the script to the end. There is no hurry and no need to jump to conclusions.

Through decatastrophizing or playing the entire script, you can learn to think differently when faced with emotional situations, offer emotional regulation and generally reduce anxiety and catastrophic thinking.

Important Tips

- ***Take a step back:*** Instead of focusing on the worst-case scenario, take a step back and see how similar situations have previously played out.

- ***Recognize that catastrophizing is negative:*** You may take catastrophizing as a way of protecting yourself from danger and problems. While, in some cases, anxiety does that, there is nothing positive about catastrophizing. You have to focus and respond to the situation on the ground, not build up scenarios in your head.

- ***Recognize those negative thoughts:*** A simple way of doing this is by asking yourself if your thoughts are appropriate and realistic as per the situation.

- ***Bring out the evidence:*** Some catastrophic thoughts can be relentless, so bring out the evidence. You can ask yourself based on experience the likelihood of your worry becoming true. For example, if someone doesn't want to have coffee with another, they decline. Acceptance means willingness.

- ***Maintain perspective:*** You have to focus on the reality and maintain that perspective. Ask yourself how you will feel in a week's time or more, depending on the situation.

- ***Imagine and visualize:*** Looking ahead is important. Imagine having that coffee with that colleague and the conversation. You can also detach yourself from the situation and imagine offering advice to a friend and looking back at this in the future after the event has happened. We tend to be kinder to others, and so it helps if you give your place to someone else, then you can see things more clearly.

Steps in decatastrophizing

1. Generate alternative explanations

Instead of only focusing on the worst-case scenario, give it some siblings to play with. Ideally, you should develop three scenarios: the worst-case scenario, the best-case scenario, and then the most-likely scenario.

You already have the worst-case scenario that your mind has labored tirelessly over, so it is time to develop the best-case scenario. Put effort in making it as humorous, happy, lavish, perfect, light and fun as you possibly can. It should be a complete opposite of the worst-case scenario.

For the most-likely scenario, think as realistically as you can, considering the best-case and the worst-case scenario. You can use previous experience to make up this scenario.

You will realize that you are already feeling better since you have allowed yourself to see other possibilities.

2. Assess probabilities

Look at those scenarios in earnest and assess the probability of their actually happening. You will realize that the best-case scenario and the worst-case scenario both have a low probability of coming true, usually less than 5%. The highest probability goes to the most-likely scenario. Life is usually not that extreme.

3. Develop a coping strategy

Since you may not be fully convinced that the worst-case scenario will not happen and justifiably so, there is still a 5% probability. You may feel better if you have a coping strategy to deal with the unlikely occurrence of the worst-case scenario. Alternatively, you can skip this step.

Come up with measures to implement if the worst-case situation occurs. Being prepared will reduce stress and anxiety and stop those thoughts from haunting you.

Over time, you can break the habit of catastrophizing simply by allowing the script to run till the end without jumping to conclusions. Go for the coffee date and see how it goes, instead of making up thousands of scenarios and reasons why it will be a disaster. It could be what you needed to unwind, and you could end up with great insights that make your work better.

Chapter Summary

In this chapter, you have learned about another CBT technique, called playing the entire script. In particular, you have learned that:

- You do not need to jump to conclusions about the situation. Instead of thinking of the worst-case scenario, let the entire script play out.
- Developing a coping strategy could help those who cannot seem to find peace by preparing them for its unlikely occurrence.
- Catastrophizing is negative.

Final Words

The world of mental illnesses can be dark, gloomy and lonely. You may feel like you do not want to go on with life, especially when dealing daily with stress, anxiety, depression and intrusive thoughts. However, it is time to be courageous and resolve to get better. I did it. I started on the journey to health, wellness, peace and calm, albeit reluctantly. Here I am today: whole, energized, healthy and glowing with inner peace.

As we have seen in this book, there are some easy CBT techniques that we can use to make our lives better. Of course, it is important to see a therapist or a mental-health professional who will do an assessment and provide a diagnosis of what ails you, enabling you to take action. While there are different treatment methods, I find that Cognitive Behavioral Therapy works the best. In addition to being very effective, you can complete it in a short time, you can practice most of the techniques at home, and you can work by refocusing your thoughts, emotions and behavior in a manner that gets rid of the negative ones and welcomes positivity.

The first step in addressing mental-health disorders is to ensure safety. You may have had the thought of how liberating it would be to check out of this world and leave all the suffering and hopelessness behind. You are not alone, I attempted to do so. But you do not have to. Instead, focus on creating a safety plan. If you don't do anything else, create a safety plan. You will be able to know when things are spiraling out of control and know what to do about it. Having this plan does not make you vulnerable, no, it makes you prepared for the extremely dark days. You are less likely to give in to those harmful thoughts when you have a plan and follow it.

We have looked at 11 techniques that you can use either at home or in therapy with a qualified mental-health professional. If you look keenly at these techniques, you will notice that they are simple and easy to apply. You can exercise mindfulness in your daily activities, you can role-play in front of your mirror and you can easily subdivide overwhelming tasks even in the comfort of your home or in traffic. There are also many ways of taking the stress off and have some fun to keep the mood light and positivity up. You can have fun with your friends, laugh, play a game or any other activity that makes you feel good. You can also find ways to relax, like going for a massage, lighting candles, listening to smooth music or taking a walk.

For you to see the effectiveness of these techniques, it is important that you are committed to the process. You are not likely to see results in a day. Besides, the beginning is always the hardest. You will have to be willing to step out of your comfort zone and take action. If you choose to schedule activities that make you feel better, you have to follow through and attend those events. There is no wishing the negative thoughts away. You have to get up and work toward a better mental health. The good news is that it gets better with time. As you progress with whichever technique you choose, you will realize that it becomes a part of you. You will be mindful of eating in no time, you will embrace relaxation and fun. You will appreciate cognitive restructuring and note how easy you can identify a negative thought and immediately replace it with a positive one. Your mood will lift, you will laugh and love more. All the simple exercises will make your body strong and beautiful, while your mind will be a power to reckon with. No longer will you be hiding away in your blanket, afraid to draw the curtains and face a new day. Instead, you will wake up energized and ready to tackle whatever challenge the world throws at you, and it will. You will ooze of positivity and will look forward to a long, joyful and successful life.

Choose techniques that work with whatever shortcomings that you may have or use a combination of technique to cover a large base. If you find that a technique is not working effectively for you, don't struggle. Adopt another one. CBT works at reducing your anxiety, stress and intrusive thoughts, not increasing them. Take things easy, but be eager to learn, grow and feel better. Remember that you are making all the effort for your own good, to have a quality life and enjoy it with those around you.

Do not allow mental illnesses to intimidate you, you can overcome through Cognitive Behavioral Therapy. There is hope for a fuller better life!

"Change your thoughts and you will
change your world."
— Anonymous

Thank you,
Michael B. Stump

Free Bonus

— ◆ ◇ ◆ —

Overcome Anxiety Book

How To Stop The Cycle Of Anxiety, Worry & Fear So
You Can Regain Control Of Your Life Forever

Scan The Code To Get This FREE Book.

(Your mobile camera has a built-in scanner.)

Printed in Great Britain
by Amazon

65192753R00099